Berlitz®

D1329246

Sicily

Berlitz
Sicily

Text by Stephen Brewer
Updated by Geoffrey Aquilina Ross
Photography: Chris Coe, except 24, 26, 56 and
65 by Gregory Wrona
Cover photograph: Chris Coe
Layout: Media Content Marketing, Inc.
Cartography by Raffaele De Gennaro
Managing Editor: Tony Halliday

Second Edition 2003 (Updated 2007)

CONTACTING THE EDITORS
Every effort has been made to provide accurate information in this publication, but
changes are inevitable. The publisher cannot be responsible for any resulting loss,
inconvenience or injury. We would appreciate it if readers would call our attention
to any errors or outdated information by contacting Berlitz Publishing, PO Box 7910,
London SE1 1WE, England. Fax: (44) 20 7403 0290;
e-mail: berlitz@apaguide.co.uk; www.berlitzpublishing.com

CONTENTS

● A (☛) in the text denotes a highly recommended sight

Sicily

INTRODUCTION

When Sicilians make the 3-km (2-mile) trip across the Strait of Messina, they are likely to say that they are going to Italy. Italians on the peninsula, for that matter, tend to think of their neighbours in Sicily as foreigners, or at least as being a bit foreign, and this is a distinction with which few Sicilians would take issue.

Travellers will quickly notice that Sicily feels different from any place else in Italy or other parts of Europe. To understand why, you only need to look to the past. The events of history have left a distinct imprint on Sicily and it is in evidence everywhere on the island. Just about all the powers that prowled the Mediterranean over the past 3,000 years set their sights on Sicily, and they left behind many stunning relics of their presence.

The juxtaposition of classical temples, mosaic-filled churches and ornate piazzas lends a theatrical and decidedly unique presence to the island. In Palermo, the cathedral that the Spanish so richly ornamented is only steps away from the mosaic-filled palace that was the seat of the enlightened courts of the island's Saracen and Norman rulers; the Baroque churches and piazzas of Catania incorporate columns of Roman temples; medieval Erice is built near the site of a temple allegedly built by some of the island's earliest settlers, the Elymians.

Many islanders still speak Sicilian, a combination of words and sounds from the long Greek, Latin, Aragonese, Arabic and Norman-French past; Sicilian is as foreign to an Italian from north of the strait as it is to someone who doesn't speak a word of Italian. The food in Sicily is different from that of the mainland, too; the lemons, capers and almonds that the Arabs brought with them from North Africa still appear in many dishes. Since most Sicilians don't live too far from the sea, fish, often the *pesce spada* (swordfish) caught in the Strait of Messina, is a staple on most menus.

Travellers will probably notice that Sicilians approach life a little differently than other Italians do. It is difficult to quantify exactly what these differences are, but being among Sicilians is one of the pleasures of touring the island. They are welcoming to their visitors, and are likely to strike up a conversation about a son who studied in London or a cousin who lives in Chicago or Brooklyn (almost a third of the island's population emigrated in the late 19th and early 20th century). Afternoon closures, which afford shopkeepers and office workers a chance to enjoy lunch and a nap, are a little longer than they are on the mainland, usually from 1–4pm. Standing patiently in an orderly line is *not* a Sicilian characteristic; finding an occasion to socialise, whether at one of the street markets that are still the mainstay of commerce on the island or at one of the festivals that all towns and cities celebrate at some time during the year, *is* a Sicilian trait of which visitors are welcome to partake.

One reason that Sicilians don't feel the need to look beyond their shores is that the island offers plenty to keep them busy. Visitors will soon realise just how much there is to see and do on the island.

Sicily is the largest island in the Mediterranean, a hefty

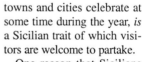

In the old town of Cefalù, locals pass the afternoon with a sociable card game.

25,708 sq km (9,926 square miles), and its landscapes of tall mountains, vast coastal plains and inland valleys are more diverse than those of many continents. The island is also remarkably rich in what can only be described as spectacle. A traveller to Sicily soon notices that the countryside, towns and monuments here are a little more extravagant than they are elsewhere.

Palermo, the capital, is on the northern coast, and Catania, the island's second largest city, is on the eastern coast. Beyond the unattractive modern outskirts of both are old centers filled with monuments that include Norman remnants in Palermo and Baroque churches and piazzas in Catania — both charged with urban vitality. These are, in fact, two of Italy's most fascinating, and often overlooked, cities. In the southeastern corner of the island is an unusually satisfying collection of cities and towns. Siracusa, the most powerful centre of Greek Sicily, is here, and its ancient ruins lie among an atmospheric Baroque city built by the Bourbons. Just inland, beyond fortifications that the Emperor Dionysius erected around the city, are towns designed in the unrestrained style known as the Sicilian Baroque. Of them, Noto takes the prize for architectural fantasy and is a stage set of curving staircases and lavish porticoes. A little deeper into the interior, in the little village of Casale near Piazza Amerina, are some of the most extensive Roman mosaics ever uncovered.

Mount Etna, Europe's most forceful volcano, is also Sicily's tallest mountain and most famous natural wonder; it dominates, and periodically threatens, the eastern coast. The Madonie are rugged mountains that rise behind the northern coast, and Capo San Vito, a rocky headland etched with beaches and secluded coves, is at the island's northwestern tip. Topping a short and by no means inclusive list of other places to include on even the briefest tour would be Agrigento, Selinunte and Segesta, with the largest and best-preserved Greek temples on the island; these monuments are especially evocative because they stand next to blue seas and are surrounded by olive trees, jasmine and wild fennel. The volcano on Stromboli, one of the Aeolian Islands that float off the northern coast, can be counted on to provide a round-the-clock performance; it sends fiery lava down the mountainside into the hissing sea about every half hour.

Cefalù, on the northern coast, and Taormina, on the eastern coast, are justifiably the island's most popular seaside resorts. Aside from their beaches, these pleasant towns also throw in some remarkable monuments: a Greek theatre and medieval palaces in Taormina, a Norman cathedral and an Arabic old town in Cefalù. Erice, on the west coast, is the most dramatically poised town on the island, atop the rocky escarpment of a tall mountain high above windmill-studded salt pans and the sea.

Travellers will also come to Sicily with some notions of the island's ongoing woes, most notably the activities of the Mafia, or Cosa Nostra. Despite some recent government intervention and opposition from ordinary citizens, the Mafia is very much a presence in Sicily, though one that probably won't be noticed by visitors. What is obvious is the unregulated building that has fattened Mafia coffers in recent years. In cities elsewhere in Italy, modern housing and industrial zones are usually carefully planned so that they don't intrude on historic centers and rural landscapes. Cities in Sicily, unfortunately, are often ringed with uncontrolled modern building put up with little regard for the environs. Even some of the vista of the temples at Agrigento has been marred by illegal modern construction..

There are, however, signs of improvement. In recent years Palermitani and Catanese have been busy restoring their churches and palaces (and many may be closed as a result). The government has set the Madonie mountains, Capo San Vito and other beautiful landscapes aside as protected reserves.

A traveller will have to determine how best to partake of Sicily's plentitude of riches. A first-time visitor may want to make a circuit of the island in order to take in a broad swath of Sicily's sights. A few suggestions on places to base yourself en route: Palermo is well-situated for exploring the western half of the island and offers good public transportation to places even as far afield as Segesta, Cefalù and the Madonie mountains; from Taormina you can easily

On a break from their scooter ride, a couple enjoys the sanctuary of a Palermo park.

make excursions to Catania and Mount Etna; Siracusa puts the Baroque towns of the southeast within easy reach; from Agrigento, Piazza Armerina and the mosaics at Casale can easily be reached by train and bus or by car; and Erice is a nice spot from which to explore Marsala, Mozia and Capo San Vito. Of course, you'll also want to board a boat in Milazzo for a trip out to the Aeolian islands, or from Trapani to the Egadi islands or Pantelleria.

You'll also come upon places that will lure you to throw the itinerary to the winds and settle in for a spell. Especially tempting in this regard are the whitewashed, Arabic old town of Cefalù; any number of quiet Aeolian islands; the view-graced theatre in Taormina; the seaside temples at Selinunte; and the quiet streets of medieval Erice. If you have to press on, don't be too upset. In Sicily, things tend to stay around for a very long time.

A BRIEF HISTORY

All roads may lead to Rome, but for much of recorded history all sea lanes have led to Sicily. The island's position in the middle of the Mediterranean has been both the proverbial curse and a blessing. Sicilians haven't enjoyed too many centuries of peace, but the various powers that have coveted their island over the centuries have left behind a heady mix of cultures and riches.

Ever since the Phoenicians began pulling ashore sometime around the 8th century BC, many of the powers of the Mediterranean and European worlds have fought for a stake in Sicily. The Greeks, Romans and Carthaginians turned the island into one of the great battlefields of ancient times; the Normans routed the Saracens, and the Spanish stepped in to replace the French.

This long history is so much in evidence in Sicily that a visitor comes away from the island with a far-reaching overview of Western civilisation. The Phoenicians left a remarkable settlement, Mozia, on the little island of San Pantaleo, off the western coast. Sicily's Greek cities, especially those at Siracusa, Agrigento, Selinunte and Segesta, provide us with some of the most extensive and best-preserved architectural remnants to come down from the classical age. Sumptuous mosaics at Casale (Piazza Amerina) are just some of the many remains of the Romans, who were here until the last days of the Empire. The Cappella Palatina in Palermo and the cathedral at Monreale (in the hills above the capital) show off the considerable achievements of the Normans, who came to Sicily from the lands of northern France. The Castello Ursino in Catania is an example of the fortifications required to defend a foothold in Sicily during the Middle Ages.

Early Settlers

Long before these empires began to establish strongholds in Sicily, Paleolithic and Neolithic peoples were occupying settlements scattered across the island. The cave paintings on Levanzo, in the Egadi Islands, are thought to be at least 10,000 years old. By the 10th century BC, a tribe known as the Sicili had migrated from mainland Italy to Sicily, giving the island its name. The Sicili settled in the east; the Sicani, from North Africa, and the Elymians, thought to have descended from the Trojans, established themselves in the west.

Sometime around the 8th century BC, Phoenicians sailed from the shores of the eastern Mediterranean to establish outposts at Mozia and elsewhere in Sicily. The Greeks, who would eventually overpower all these cultures, began arriving about the same time. Most of the Greek settlers came in search of land to farm, and Sicily offered vast tracts of fertile soil and ideal growing conditions. From colonies in Siracusa and elsewhere along the east coast, the Greeks spread across the island, establishing colonies at Gela, Agrigento and Selinunte. Agrigento, known to the ancients as Agras, became especially powerful, and enough is left of this city on the southern coast to suggest the extent of its wealth. However, Siracusa soon became the supreme power on Sicily.

The Greek Centuries

In 480BC, the armies of the various Greek colonies joined forces under Gelon, the tyrannical ruler of Siracusa, to defeat the Carthaginians at Himera, on Sicily's northern coast. The Greek victory ensured the supremacy of Siracusa in the affairs of Sicily until the city fell to the Romans some 250 years later. The victory also assured that Sicily would become a major Greek power in the Mediterranean; in fact, Sicily and the

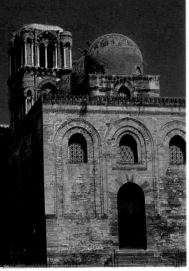

The domes of San Cataldo and La Martorana — landmarks since the 12th century.

southern Italian mainland became known as Magna Graecia (Greater Greece) and had a larger Greek population than Greece itself.

Greek dominance, however, didn't bring an end to warfare. The colonies often fought among themselves. Segesta, an Athenian satellite on the northwestern coast, was almost continually at war with Selinunte, an ally of Siracusa on the southern coast. Athens was alarmed by the ambitions of Siracusa and saw an opportunity to attack when Segesta asked for help in repelling the attacks from Selinunte. Athens assembled a massive fleet and sailed to Sicily in 415BC; the so-called Great Expedition ended in a humiliating defeat for the Athenians. The Siracusans imprisoned some 7,000 Athenian soldiers and put them to work in its limestone quarries, the Latomie.

Carthage, the colony the Phoenicians settled on the north shore of Africa near modern-day Tunis, wasn't as easy to quell. The Carthaginian general Hannibal attacked Selinunte, Agrigento and other Sicilian cities; Siracusa's tyrannical ruler, Dionysius I, retaliated in 397BC by leveling Mozia, the Carthaginian stronghold on the island. Under Agathocles, Sicilian troops crossed the Mediterranean and attacked the Carthaginians on their own turf.

In the 3rd century BC, Sicily became the battleground of the Punic Wars that broke out between Rome and Carthage. When Siracusa sided with the Carthaginians in the Second Punic War, Rome sacked the city in 211BC and took control of the island. The Roman Empire continued to control Sicily for the next seven centuries.

Romans and Saracens

For Rome, Sicily was one vast wheat field, supplying the Empire with grain. Slaves from Rome's other Mediterranean conquests were brought to Sicily to clear and work the land; they revolted against harsh conditions twice, in 139BC and 104BC, and were harshly suppressed both times. For the most part, though, Roman rule brought a commodity that until then was unknown in Sicily — peace — as well as the amphitheaters, baths and other Roman structures that still stand around the island.

Christianity arrived in Sicily around AD200, and Siracusa became one of the most fervent early Christian strongholds in the Mediterranean. Until the Emperor Constantine lifted the prohibition against Christians a century later, thousands of Siracusans worshipped and buried their dead in catacombs beneath the city. Not

Frescoes at Palermo's Galleria Regionale highlight Sicily's religious history.

long after Rome fell to the Visigoths in 410, Sicily became prey to Vandals and Ostrogoths who sacked the coasts. By 535 the island had fallen into the hands of the Byzantines; Siracusa was capital of the Eastern Byzantine Empire for five years, from 663 to 668.

The next wave of invasion came from North Africa. The island of Pantelleria, where an Arabic influence is still much in evidence, fell first in 700. It wasn't until the 9th century when the assault began in force. After decades of fighting, the so-called Saracens — including Arabs, Spanish Muslims and Berbers — took Palermo in 831 and Siracusa in 878. Arab rule ushered in another golden age for Sicily. Palermo became one of the largest and most cosmopolitan cities in the world, comparable to Constantinople and Baghdad. The Muslim rulers revitalised the countryside, building irrigation systems and introducing oranges and lemons to the landscape.

The rich mosaics at the Villa Romana outside Piazza Armerina provide evidence of the Roman presence.

Once again, the prosperity of Sicily proved to be irre-sistible to other powers. This time it was a Norman lord, Roger de Hauteville, who set his sights on the island. With a small army of knights, Roger took Messina in 1061. All of Sicily was under Norman rule by 1091, with Palermo as its

Masters of a Sicilian Style

While the achievements of Greeks and Normans are often what captures a visitor's attention, Sicilian artists have made considerable contributions of their own; several artists developed a distinctly Sicilian style in their work. You will encounter them frequently in your travels around the island.

Domenico Gagini (1448–1492) came to Palermo in 1458 and spent the rest of his life gracing churches with his elegant Madonnas and other sculptures; his son, **Antonello** (1478–1536), carried on the tradition to become Sicily's foremost sculptor of the Renaissance. You will find their work in numerous churches and in Palermo's Galleria Regionale della Sicilia, where a room is filled with Gagini masterpieces.

Rosario Gagliardi (1700–1770) is the architect who created many of the Baroque churches and public buildings that transform towns like Noto and Ragusa into stage sets. The church of San Giorgio in Ragusa is a fine example of his mastery of this whimsical style.

Antonello da Messina (1430–1479) studied in Naples and Venice and returned to Sicily to perfect a unique style that puts him among the masters of Renaissance painting. He combined a mastery of light and spatial depth to create such masterpieces as his *Portrait of an Unknown Man*, now in the Museo Mandralisca in Cefalù.

Giacomo Serpotta (1656–1732) perfected the art of stucco work, or molded plaster. His creations, which adorn the Oratorio del Rosario di San Domenico and other oratorios in Palermo, cover the walls with delicate religious imagery.

capital and Roger, now known as Count Roger of Sicily, as its ruler. Rather than impose a foreign yoke on the island, Roger accommodated the island's rich Greek, Roman, Byzantine and Roman heritage; Norman art and architecture, so richly preserved in the Norman churches in Palermo, Monreale and Cefalù, displays this fusion. When Roger's son was crowned Roger II, King of Sicily, in 1130, his holdings included Sicily and most of southern Italy and his court was one of the wealthiest and most cosmopolitan in the world.

Stupor Mundi and the Sicilian Vespers

A descendant, Frederick II von Hohenstaufen, was to carry on the Norman tradition of enlightened rule when he took the crown in 1220. His mother was Catherine, Roger II's daughter, and his father was Henry VI of Swabia; this heritage gave him control of Sicily, much of Italy and parts of Germany. He introduced a unified legal system, promoted the arts and sciences and encouraged a blending of Islamic, Jewish and Christian cultures. Frederick ruled for more than 40 years and became known as *Stupor Mundi*, Wonder of the World.

Frederick's death once again left Sicily up for grabs. Among the contenders was the Papacy, eager to get control of the lands of southern Italy. Backed by Pope Urban IV, Charles of Anjou, brother of the French King Saint Louis, defeated the Hohenstaufen supporters in a series of battles and became King of Sicily and Naples in 1268. Determined to punish Sicily for its loyalty to the Hohenstaufens, Charles imposed heavy taxes and confiscated lands.

An uprising against French rule broke out in Palermo on 30 March 1282; the first shots rang out at the hour the bells of the church of Santo Spirito rang for Vespers, and the revolt has come to be known as the Sicilian Vespers. Charles' repressive measures certainly account in part for the insurrection. Some scholars claim that it was instigated by the Byzantine Emperor Michael VIII; he had learned that Charles was plotting to attack Constantinople and wrest control of Byzantine lands and wished to divert the French by keeping them busy in Sicily. The immediate cause was an incident in which a French soldier stopped a Sicilian bride on her way to church and searched her for concealed weapons. An angry crowd killed the soldier immediately, and within days the citizenry had slaughtered more than 8,000 French troops across the island.

Ancient Palermo offers many artistic reminders of Sicily's variegated past.

King Peter III of Aragón (whose wife, Constance, was a Hohenstaufen) arrived in a flotilla five months later, and the Sicilian nobles offered the Spaniard the throne. The Angevins and the Aragonese skirmished for control of the island for the next 20 years, and in the end Sicily belonged to the Spanish — and would remain in their hands for the next 400 years.

Spanish Rule

Sicily became more or less a backwater when the European powers directed their expansionist ambitions to the New World. This inattention ensured that Sicily enjoyed one of the few peri-

Historical Highlights

Before 10,000BC Paleolithic and Neolithic peoples settle in Egadi Islands

10th century BC Sicili, Sicani and Elymians settle in Sicily

8th century BC Phoenicians establish outposts at Mozia; Greek colonists settle in Gela, Agrigento and Selinunte

480BC Greeks defeat the Carthaginians at Himera, ensuring Greek supremacy over the island with Siracusa as most powerful city

415BC Athenians launch so-called Great Expedition to take Siracusa and are defeated

397BC Siracusa's tyrannical ruler, Dionysius I, levels Mozia

211BC In aftermath of Second Punic War, Rome sacks Siracusa and takes control of Sicily

About 200AD Early Christianity takes hold in Sicily

5th century Vandals and Ostrogoths attack Sicilian coast settlements

663–668 Siracusa is capital of eastern Byzantine Empire

Around 700 Arabs invade island of Pantelleria

9th century Saracens take Palermo in 831 and Siracusa in 878 to rule Sicily

11th century Roger de Hauteville captures Messina in 1061 and brings all of Sicily under Norman rule by 1091

1220 Frederick II von Hohenstaufen, of Norman and Swabian heritage, takes the crown and brings 40 years of enlightened rule to Sicily

1268 Charles of Anjou, brother of the French King Louis, becomes King of Sicily and Naples

30 March 1282 In an uprising known as the Sicilian Vespers, citizens rebel against repressive French rule; a Spaniard, King Peter III of Aragón, takes the throne to begin 400 years of Spanish rule

1669 Mount Etna erupts and lava flows through the streets of Catania

1693 An earthquake flattens many cities in the southeast; in rebuilding them, architects perfect a flamboyant style known as the Sicilian Baroque

18th century Sicily passes to the House of Savoy, then to the Austrians, and goes to the Spanish house of Bourbon in 1734

11 May 1860 Freedom fighter Giuseppe Garibaldi sails into Marsala; Sicilians depose the Bourbons and become part of the new Kingdom of Italy

Late 19th–early 20th centuries Many Sicilians emigrate to escape widespread poverty

July 1943 Allies make first European landings of World War II in Sicily

1950s–present Italy's postwar economic boom brings some improvements but unemployment remains high

1980s–1990s Mafia violence triggers government crackdown and citizen movements against organized crime

2005 Plans are confirmed for a 4-km (2½-mile) suspension bridge to link Sicily to mainland Italy.

The Greek temple of Segesta stands as one of the best-preserved architectural specimens from the classical age.

ods of long peace in its history. In the absence of human drama, nature stepped in. The plague, brought to Sicily by the ships that called at its harbors, broke out repeatedly and decimated large portions of the population.

The end of the 17th century was especially calamitous. Mount Etna erupted in 1669 and sent molten lava flowing through the streets of Catania and other towns and cities on the eastern coast. An earthquake in 1693, also centered in the east, was even more destructive and took an enormous toll on human life. Sicilians rebuilt Noto and other cities in a distinctive style, the Sicilian Baroque.

The now peaceful Aeolian Islands were for centuries vital to military strategies.

The Treaty of Utrecht divided Spanish holdings, and in the early 18th century Sicily once again became a pawn of foreign powers. The island passed from the Italian House of Savoy to the Austrians and, in 1734, back to the Spanish, this time to the Bourbons. The British convinced the Bourbon king Ferdinand I to introduce a constitution, but he soon repealed it and called in Austrian mercenaries when citizens took to the streets of Palermo and other cities calling for independence; his successor, Ferdinand II, bombarded Messina in 1848 to quell an uprising for independence there.

From Unification into the Present

This unrest set the stage for Giuseppe Garibaldi, the freedom fighter and a leader of the Risorgimento, the campaign for the unification of Italy. He sailed into Marsala on 11 May 1860 with his so-called Thousand, a reference to the guerrilla army that accompanied him. Garibaldi's soldiers and Sicilian partisans were soon fighting in the streets of Palermo, and the island was free of Bourbon rule within a year. Sicilians voted overwhelmingly to join the new Kingdom of Italy, but many were soon disillusioned — widespread poverty and government repression made life as part of a unified Italy more difficult than it had been under the Bourbons.

For many Sicilians, the only escape from impoverishment was emigration. By 1914, more than a million and a half Sicilians had left the island, usually for North and South America. The reforms introduced later by Mussolini and his fascist government did little to alleviate poverty, illiteracy and unemployment in Sicily.

The island once again became a battleground in World War II. In July 1943, the Allies made their first European landings at Gela on the southern coast. Allied bombardments flattened Messina, where the German defensive was entrenched. Other cities were not spared. In fact, parts of Palermo are still strewn with rubble from World War II bombings, largely because government funds for rebuilding have been misappropriated by corrupt officials who are often linked with the Mafia.

The Mafia took root in Sicily in the 1860s, ostensibly to help the rural poor get their share of the land reform and other benefits that were to accompany freedom from foreign rule. In effect, the Mafia became an integral part of the island's power structure, controlling business and the workings of government, and today is said to ensure that Sicily remains a centre for drug trafficking. The Mafia's highly placed government

23

The vibrant capital city of Palermo at night.

links have included Giulio Andreotti, the former prime minister. Journalists, judges and officials who have worked against the organisation have routinely been murdered; Giovanni Falcone, one of the most vocal and effective anti-Mafia crusaders, was killed in a bombing in 1992. Attempts to crack down on Mafia operations have only occasionally been effective, but the battle continues. Trials in 1997 sent several Mafia bosses to prison for the murder of Falcone. Some of the most effective anti-Mafia forces are ordinary citizens speaking out against organised crime. The progress that has been made was highlighted by the opening of an anti-Mafia museum in Corleone, the heart of Mafia territory, in 2000.

Another force at work in Sicily since World War II has been the so-called 'Italian Miracle', the economic progress that has made Italy the world's eighth wealthiest nation. Like the rest of the South, Sicily has been bypassed by many of the new jobs and big salaries, but the standard of living has improved. Your first impressions of Sicily may well be of industrial plants, huge tracts of unattractive modern housing, and highways that often mar the countryside, all the products of recent prosperity. Press on, though, because at the heart of just about every city and town in Sicily lies an old centre that bears the marks of centuries of fascinating history.

WHERE TO GO

T he easiest way to see a good measure of Sicily's cities, ruins, beaches and other attractions is to circle the coast and make occasional forays into the interior and to nearby islands. We begin in Palermo, and head east to begin a tour.

PALERMO

Palermo does not readily enchant its visitors. The chaotic capital of Sicily is noisy and traffic-filled, riddled with decay in parts, overbuilt with concrete in others. But take some time to settle into Palermo. Walk the narrow streets and alleys of the old city. You'll discover Norman palaces, Baroque churches, chapels shimmering in mosaics, outdoor markets overflowing with olives and blood oranges, quaint puppet theatres and grandiose oratories, and smoothing out the rough edges, a great deal of warm-hearted street life. The city's setting, in the valley known as the Conca d'Oro, beside the Gulf of Palermo and beneath the flanks of Monte Pellegrino, is beautiful.

The Quattro Canti and Environs

The **Quattro Canti**, or Four Corners, is the centre of the old city; most of Palermo's sights are an easy walk from this busy crossroads at the intersection of the Via Maqueda and the Corso Vittorio Emanuele. The façades of the buildings on each corner — three Baroque palaces and the church of **San Giuseppe dei Teatini** — are ornamented with fountains, and each is also embellished with statuary that represents a season, one of four Spanish kings of Sicily and the patron saint of one of the four quarters that surround the Quattro Canti. If the church is open, step inside for a look at the angels, stuccoes, frescoes and other ornamentation that are typical of the Sicilian Baroque.

Piazza Pretoria, filled with the statues of Fontana Pretoria.

Piazza Pretoria is just a few steps south along Via Maqueda. The **Fontana Pretoria** takes up most of the square and is more commonly known as the Fontana della Vergogna, or Fountain of Shame — this is a reference to the seeming licentiousness of the naked figures who frolic in the spray. Garibaldi is said to have sat on the edge of the fountain during the fierce battles of 1870, instilling the citizenry with the courage to fight on for independence. Flanking one side of the square is the **Palazzo delle Aquile**, the town hall, named for the stone eagles that cover its façade. The other massive presence is the church of **Santa Caterina**; behind its austere façade is another Baroque interior, covered with brightly coloured frescoes and plasterwork angels that tumble from every surface.

The Piazza Bellini, just a few steps to the east, is graced with the three small red domes of the chapel of **San Cataldo** and the 12th-century campanile of **La Martorana**. San Cataldo is squat and plain, and aside from its mosaic flooring, was left undecorated when its founder, a chancellor of

William I, died in 1160. La Martorana is more elaborate, and was founded by George of Antioch, Roger II's chief minister, in 1146 as a seat of the Greek Orthodox church. Despite a Baroque restoration that added the cupids around the entryway, much of the Norman mosaic work remains intact. The gold, green and azure tiles of the dome depict Christ flanked by saints and prophets, and a nearby mosaic of Christ crowning Roger II is said to be a reliable likeness of the Norman king.

The Albergheria

The streets and alleys of the Albergheria quarter stretch south and west of Piazza Bellini. Via Maqueda and Via Bosco lead into the centre of the quarter, the Piazza Carmine, passing stately palaces, worn centuries-old buildings that show their age and rubble-filled craters left by World War II bombings. The stalls of a daily fruit and vegetable market fill Piazza Carmine, the adjacent Piazza Ballarò and the surrounding streets. Above this busy scene rises the green-and-white dome of **Chiesa del Gesù**, founded in late 16th century as the first Jesuit church in Sicily, and that of the church of the **Carmine**. While the interior of Il Gesù is another swirl of Baroque excess, that of the Carmine is vast and far more sedate.

> A good term to know when visiting churches in Sicily is *'Chiuso per restauro'*, closed for restoration, which many are.

The Cattedrale and Palazzo dei Normanni

From Quattro Canti, Corso Vittorio Emanuele leads west past old-fashioned shops and Baroque palaces to several of Palermo's most important monuments. The **Cattedrale** was begun in 1185 but not completed, with the addition of its dome, until 1801. As a result, the building is an incongruous mixture of styles: the 12th-century towers are Norman, the façade and south porch are Gothic and the interior is coldly Neoclassical.

The church is a pantheon of the Normans, who came to Sicily in 1061, routed the Arabs and ruled the island ably for a century. Roger II, the Norman king who made the island the centre of the Mediterranean World, is interred here among his royal relations against his will; he wanted to be buried in the cathedral he built in Cefalù *(see page 41)*. In the adjacent Treasury, Constance of Aragon's bejeweled crown is on display alongside rings and other artifacts removed from the royal tombs during a 19th-century rearrangement. Of a more macabre nature are the relics of several saints, including a withered extremity said to be the foot of Mary Magdalen.

The **Palazzo dei Normanni**, or Palazzo Reale, was actually built by Sicily's Arab rulers in the ninth century. Under both the Arabs and the Normans, Palermo was one of the largest and most civilised cities in the world and the palace was a centre of the arts and learning.

Little of the Arab and Norman palace remains. The façade that overlooks the old city is a 17th-century addition made by the island's Spanish rulers, and many of the salons and lesser quarters are now occupied by Sicily's regional government. One stunning Norman remnant, however, is the **Cappella Palatina**, the exquisite chapel commissioned by Roger II. Mosaics cover every surface, depicting the tales of the Old and New Testaments in a frank, charming style that infuses the softly lit space with a sense of faith and earnest artistry executed for love of God and a just ruler. The scenes are not, however, entirely of a spiritual nature — several panels depict life at court, including a picnic in Roger's harem, and provide a look at the brilliant mingling of Arab and Western traditions that flourished under the Normans.

The Palazzo dei Normanni reflects Sicily's various rulers since its construction by the Arabs in the 9th century.

Capping the glittering profusion of gold and silver tiles is a purely Arab touch, a honeycombed, wooden ceiling.

A marble staircase leads from the chapel to the Royal Apartments, a collection of chambers stuffily decorated in the ornate tastes of later centuries. The best room, in a small wing of the original Norman palace, is the Sala di Re Ruggero. The walls are covered in mosaics of hunting scenes and exotic landscapes in which lions and camels roam among palms.

San Giovanni degli Eremiti

Another remnant of Norman Palermo, the now-deconsecrated church of **San Giovanni degli Eremiti**, is just south of the palace on Via dei Benedittini. While the interior is stark and devoid of elaborate decoration, this five-domed Norman-Arab church is beautiful in its simplicity and is surrounded by gardens and cloisters planted with palms, cactus and jasmine. The **Parco d'Orleans** across the street is named for the one-time resident of the palace it surrounds, Louis-Philippe

d'Orléans. He was exiled here in 1809 in the aftermath of the Paris Commune and later returned to France to become King; the palace is now the residence of the president of Sicily.

From the Vucciria to Piazza Verdi

Corso Vittorio Emanuele leads northeast from Quattro Canti towards the sea and several other quarters of old Palermo. Just a few blocks from the Quattro Canti, the Corso crosses Via Roma, which slightly

Make your own discoveries of ancient relics at the Museo Archeologico Regionale.

north skirts the **Vucciria**, Palermo's busiest market. Steps descend into a warren of stalls, from which you might emerge with a religious medallion or two, an espresso maker, an octopus, some sea urchins and a swordfish, and bags filled with the capers, olives, lemons and other produce that grow in such abundance across Sicily. (To ensure that you also leave the market with your valuables, take precautions against pickpockets and jewellery snatchers.)

A few blocks north of the market, Via Roma comes to **Piazza San Domenico**, an airy square dominated by the 18th-century façade of the church of the same name. Behind the church is the remarkable **Oratorio del Rosario**. Some of Palermo's best Baroque artistry decorates small chapels like this one, in which stucco cherubs and other figures cover every inch of the walls. The Rosario is the finest of all, since its exuberance is the work of the master of Baroque decoration, Giacomo Serpotta, a native of Palermo. The altarpiece is a rich depiction of the Virgin of the Rosary by Van Dyck; the Dutch painter came to work in Palermo's churches sometime around 1628, but he left when the plague broke out and completed this painting in Genoa.

More of the friezes that emerged from Serpotta's fertile imagination and skilled hands also decorate the **Oratorio di Santa Cita**, a few blocks north on Via Squarcialpo. Stucco angels surround frescoed stories from the New Testament and spectacular scenes depicting the victory of the Christian fleets over the Turks at the Battle of Lepanto.

The Museo Archeologico

The **Museo Archeologico Regionale** is on the other side of Via Roma. In rooms surrounding the two cloisters of a former monastery, some of the most important pieces unearthed in Sicily are displayed alongside finds from elsewhere in the ancient world: painting fragments from Pompeii, Roman bronzes, Greek vases, a room floored with Roman mosaics uncovered in Palermo and an extensive collection of Etruscan urns and tombs, found in Tuscany.

The prizes, though, are the pieces from Selinunte, the ruined city on Sicily's southwestern coast *(see page 71)*. A famed collection of metopes, the stone carvings that adorned the tops of the temples, are towards the back of the museum in the **Sala di Selinunte**. Several figures from Greek mythology appear on the reliefs. In one, Perseus beheads Medusa, and in another, dogs set upon Acateon. On the floor above, more than 12,000 tiny figures from Selinunte's Sanctuary of Demeter are on display in the South Gallery.

Teatro Massimo

The museum is only a block east of the centre of the modern city, the Piazza Verdi. This busy piazza was laid out in the 19th century and is now surrounded by modern office blocks. At the centre of the square is the Teatro Massimo, one of the grandest opera houses in Europe. What's most remarkable about this domed Neoclassical structure is the fact that its massive doors are once again open; the theatre was hidden behind weeds and scaffolding for almost a quarter of a century. It reopened to much fanfare in 1997, exactly a hundred years after the huge stage was inaugurated with a production of Verdi's Aida.

The Kalsa

Palermo's oldest district extends southeast from the intersection of Via Roma and Corso Vittorio Emanuele. The Arabs set-

The Teatro Massimo gloriously reopened its doors in 1997 after years of neglect.

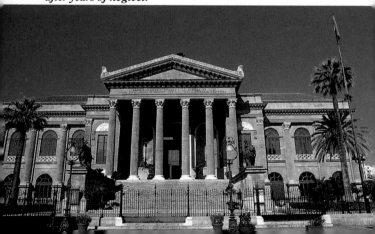

tled this seaside quarter in the 10th century, and later, Sicilian aristocrats built fine residences along the narrow streets. It's a bit difficult to imagine these more prosperous times, however, in what is now a chaotic landscape of crumbling palaces, ruined churches, flapping laundry, forbidding alleyways and extensive World War II bomb damage. Despite the general air of desolation, the neighbourhood has some fine remnants of old Palermo and a couple of excellent museums.

Exquisite works such as this mosaic fill the Galleria Regionale della Sicilia.

San Francesco and Environs

Via Paternostro leads south off the Corso to the **Chiesa di San Francesco d'Assisi**, a large Gothic structure with a sparse, stone interior that pays just tribute to Italy's patron saint. When decoration does intrude, it does so gently, most notably in the Cappella Mastrontonio; a sculpted arch by Francesco Laurana frames the entrance and is the earliest known Renaissance work in Sicily. The nearby **Oratorio di San Lorenzo**, is another masterpiece of decoration by Giacomo Serpotta. The oratorio is also famous for a lost artwork: a *Nativity* by Caravaggio, stolen in 1969 and never recovered.

The Corso continues north to the seaside, and soon skirts La Cala, the old harbour and now the moorage for the city's small fishing fleet. On the landward side rise the stately trees of **Giardino Garibaldi** and **Palazzo Chiaramonte**, most famous as the headquarters of the Inquisition from 1685 to 1782. After passing through the Porto Felice, the corso ends at the seafront and a vista of the gulf with Monte Pellegrino rising in the background.

Via Buttera, just inside the walls, is lined with some of the city's best-preserved palaces. One of them houses the **Museo Internazionale delle Marionette**, a collection of puppets that provides an introduction to this still-popular Sicilian entertainment that takes root in the island's French heritage and stars knights from the court of Charlemagne. The French Roland appears in Sicily as Orlando, and with his cohorts Rinaldo and Astolfo he engages in colourful battles against Saracen pirates, usually to defend the maiden Angelica. Performances are sometimes staged in the museum's theatre, and puppets and backdrops from Sicily and around the world are on display.

Galleria Regionale

Around the corner, on Via Alloro, is the **Galleria Regionale**, where paintings and sculpture fill the rooms of the 15th-century Palazzo Abatellis. The first floor is devoted to sculpture. Several works are by Franceso Laurana, whose sculpted archway graces the nearby church of San Francesco *(see page 34)*; his masterpiece here is a bust of Eleonora of Aragon. Another room is devoted to Antonello Gagini and other members of this family who dominated Sicilian Baroque sculpture for much of the 15th and 16th centuries. The palace chapel is decorated with *The Triumph of Death*, a fresco by an unknown artist; the eponymous subject is an archer who, from the back of a horse, launches his arrows at the noble and meek alike, sparing no one the inevitable. Sicilian paintings hang in the upstairs galleries; the most notable among them are several fine works by Antonello da Messina. A few galleries are devoted to the works of Flemish artists, whom wealthy aristocrats often brought to Palermo to paint their portraits and decorate the churches they endowed.

Take a quiet stroll through the Villa Giulia, festooned with fountains and flora.

Via Vetriera leads south from the museum to Piazza Kalsa, and just beyond this rather derelict square are two other leafy retreats. The lovely gardens of the **Villa Giulia** and the adjoining **Orto Botanico** were laid out in the late 18th century and are abloom with tropical vegetation that surrounds pools and pavilions.

Around Palermo

On the outskirts of Palermo are a number of palaces, churches and other sights; the city's efficient public transportation network puts them within easy reach of the center.

La Zisa

When the Norman King William I began to build this retreat in 1160, he fashioned the gardens and palace in the manner of an Arab pleasure pavilion. 'La Zisa' comes from the Arabic *el aziz*, or magnificent, and the mosaics, arches, fountains, vaulted ceilings and lattice windows of the three-floor palace reveal the opulence that once prevailed here. Life in the palace was made even more comfortable by fountains, pools and air vents that ensured that cool air was circulated through the many rooms in the summer (warm air in the winter). Until ongoing renovations of the grounds are complete, you are left to imagine how the palace looked when it was surrounded by lush gardens in which wild animals roamed freely. You can reach La Zisa and the Capuchin catacombs *(see below)* on bus 27 from Piazza Indipendenza.

> **Leave your valuables in the hotel safe — pickpocketing and purse snatching are fairly common in Sicily's larger cities.**

The Catacombe del Convento dei Cappuccini

In the various niches and rooms of these catacombs beneath a Capuchin monastery are the clothed corpses of 8,000 men, women and children. Many of them look remarkably alive — over the years the monks perfected a technique of injecting corpses with chemicals and dyes. The practice of preserving the dead in this fashion died out in 1920, and the last specimen to be interred here is a two-year-old girl who still looks like she's just been tucked in for a nap.

Parco della Favorita and Monte Pellegrino

On the northern edge of Palermo, the woods and formal gardens of the **Parco della Favorita** climb the lower slopes of Monte Pellegrino. Ferdinand III, Bourbon King of the Two Sicilies, chose this hilly terrain as his place of exile in 1799, and installed himself in the eccentric **Palazzina Cinese**. The palace, really an extended garden pavilion, is closed, but the former servants' quarters house the charming folk collections of the **Museo Etnografico Siciliano Pitrè**. Traditional painted carts take centre stage, though there is also a fine collection of puppets, and performances are occassionally staged. You can reach the park, which is about 3km (2 miles) from the city center, on buses 806 and 833 from Viale della Libertà.

Higher up the mountain is the **Sanctuario di Santa Rosalia**, a cave-turned-chapel that is Palermo's popular pilgrimage site. Allegedly, Palermo was saved from the plague in 1624 when Rosalia, the hermit niece of King William II, appeared to a peasant in a vision and told him to find her remains here and give her a proper burial. The plague subsided soon after Rosalia's remains were paraded through the streets en route to consecrated ground; in gratitude the citizens of Palermo chose her as their patron saint. Rosalia's cave has been fitted out with a formal Baroque foyer. Even so, and except for the addition of pews, some electric lights and hundreds of devout pilgrims, the dark interior looks much as it did when Rosalia sought refuge here. Bus 812 ascends to the sanctuary from Piazza Sturzo.

Monreale

The best example of Norman art and architecture is not in Palermo, but in this hillside town 13km (8 miles) to the southeast. William II started the town's cathedral in 1174

The Monte Pellegrino is the setting for a sanctuary and historic sites.

Palermo Churches, Museums and Other Sights

Churches and oratorios in and around Palermo are open for visits from 9am–5pm Monday–Friday, and 9am–3pm on Saturday. However there are many exceptions and some places close for lunch, so check times before you set out.

Cappella Palatina. Open Monday–Friday 9–11:45am and 3–5pm; Sunday 9–9:45am and noon–12:45pm.

Catacombe del Convento dei Cappuccini. Open daily 9am–noon, 3–5pm.

Chiesa della Martorana. Monday–Saturday 8am–1pm and 3:30–5:30pm; Sunday 8:30am–1pm.

Chiesa di San Francesco d'Assisi. Daily 7am–12:30pm and 4:30–6:30pm.

Galleria Regionale di Palazzo Abatellis. Monday–Saturday 9am–1:30pm (and 3–7:30pm Tuesday and Thursday); Sunday 9am–12:30pm.

La Zisa. Monday–Friday 9am–7pm. Sundays and public holidays 9am–1pm.

Monreale cathedral. Daily 8am–6pm.

Museo Archeologico Regionale. Monday–Saturday 8:30am–1:30pm, Tuesday and Friday also 3–7pm, Sunday 9am–1pm.

Museo Etnografico Siciliano Pitrè. Daily 9am–6pm. Closed Friday and Sunday

Palermo cathedral. Monday–Saturday 7am–7pm; Sunday 8am–1:30pm and 4–7pm; Treasury, Monday–Saturday 7–11:30am and 4–6:30pm.

Museo Internazionale delle Marionette. Monday–Friday 9am–1pm and 4–7pm; Saturday 9am–1pm. Free shows in the summer months.

San Cataldo. Monday–Friday 9am–4pm, Saturday–Sunday 9am–1pm.

Sanctuario di Santa Rosalia. Daily 7am–7pm.

San Giovanni degli Eremiti. Monday–Saturday 9am–7pm.

Villa Palagonia in Bagheria. Daily 9am–12:30pm.

— allegedly after the Madonna appeared to him in a vision and instructed him to do so, though it was more likely that he was motivated by political reasons. William had broken ties with Walter of the Mill, Bishop of Palermo. Walter was building a new church, the present-day Palermo cathedral, and William set about to outdo him. He succeeded. The **Cattedrale** in Monreale, set high above the Conca d'Oro valley and Palermo, was completed in just ten years and is one of the great monuments of the Middle Ages. Inside, the dome, walls and columns shimmer with 130 large mosaics — perhaps the finest example of mosaic art in the world. They tell the stories of the Old and New Testaments and surround a half figure of Christ that dominates the central apse. Among the many saints portrayed in the mosaics is Thomas à Becket. It was William's father-in-law, Henry II of England, who had martyred Becket but the church, meanwhile, had canonised Becket the year before the cathedral was begun, so by honouring him William was casting his allegiance with the powerful papacy. William and his father are buried in the south chapel, not far from the entrance to the **cloisters** that were part of the monastery that stood here originally. You can reach Monreale 8km (5 miles) away on bus 389 from Palermo's Piazza Indipendenza.

Bagheria

For much of the 17th and 18th century, Palermo's aristocracy built summer villas in this now suburban town, 14km (8½ miles) east of the centre and easily reached by train. Many of the villas and groves of olives and lemons that surrounded them have disappeared, but you can still get a sense of what life here was like. The only way to see many of the villas is from the road through high gates. This is not unrewarding in the case of **Villa Valguarnera** on Via Trabia; the façade is the most lavish in Bagheria, with a parapet topped by statuary.

Local fishermen still put up their modest boats on the pebble beach backed by the whitewashed town of Cefalù.

The one villa you can enter is **Villa Palagonia**, on Piazza Garibaldi. Ferdinand, Prince of Palagonia, an 18th-century resident, was a hunchback married to an adulterous wife. He decorated the gardens with more than 200 grotesque statues depicting his wife's lovers in unflattering ways, and some 65 of the caricatures remain. The interior is now fairly sedate, though in the prince's day it was filled with broken glass and piles of shattered crockery. Only in the Salone degli Specchi, where cracked mirrors are set at odd angles into the walls and ceiling, do you get a sense of the prince's bizarre tastes in interior décor.

Mondello

Palermo's most popular getaway follows a long sandy beach beneath the northern flanks of Monte Pellegrino. The rocky, forested bluffs of the mountain and the headlands of Capo Gallo at the northern end of the beach lend the town a sense of remote beauty; the fishing harbour and little lanes that wind around a medieval clock tower provide the atmosphere of a small Mediterranean fishing village, which Mondello was until about fifty years ago. The town is liveliest in the evening, when Palermitani come out to Mondello for a seaside *passeggiata* and a meal in the town's many fish restaurants. You can join them by taking bus 806 from Viale della Libertà.

EAST FROM PALERMO

The coast east of Palermo is richly endowed with old towns, ancient ruins, rugged mountains, fine beaches and, not far offshore, a volcanic archipelago. Since many of these places lie on or near the main railway lines, they can be reached easily from Palermo; or, you might consider making Cefalù your base and exploring the surrounding attractions from there.

Cefalù

Cefalù, 70km (42 miles) east of Palermo, would be a remarkable place even if it weren't for the twin-towered cathedral that rises high above its red tile roofs. This magnificent structure, founded by Roger II in 1131, is itself overshadowed by a massive crag that crowds the church and the town between a wall of rock and the sea.

> When visiting Sicily's churches, be respectful. Avoid wearing shorts, short skirts, and tops that expose your back and shoulders.

Museo Mandralisca

Allegedly, Roger was caught at sea in a storm and vowed to build a cathedral at the first harbour he came upon. That harbour was Cefalù, which by then had already witnessed the passing of the Carthaginians, Greeks, Byzantines and Arabs. Their presence is noted in the dusty collections of the **Museo Mandralisca**, where the relics on display include a rare Greek vase depicting tuna fishing in the nearby Lípari Islands. The treasure, though, is *Portrait of an Unknown Man*, Antonello da

Messina's rendering of a sly-smiled, enigmatic man who is often compared to the Mona Lisa. This collection and the palace were bestowed to the town by the 19th-century Baron Enrico Mandralisca, by all accounts a remarkable man who devoted his life to the study of natural history and archaeology (he was on the team that unearthed some of the Classical finds here) and served in the first Italian Parliament.

Piazza Duomo and the Old Town

The **cathedral** that Roger built is on the Piazza Duomo, in the centre of town. Recent restorations have stripped the church of its later Baroque decoration to show off the Byzantine mosaics to their best advantage. High above the central apse is *Christ Pantocrator*, with an elongated face and powerful eyes that seem to follow a visitor around the church; the Bible he holds is open to Latin and Greek inscriptions of 'I am the light of the world'. He is surrounded by the Virgin Mary and the twelve apostles. Among the other

With one of Sicily's finest beaches, Cefalù complements its cultural offerings with laid-back sunning and swimming.

sparse ornamentation that remains is a *Madonna and Child*, by Sicilian master Antonello Gagini.

From the piazza, narrow alleys lead into the old town and to some appealing relics of Cefalù's past. The old Greek walls provide a nice view over the sea and the town, and the *lavatoio* is a wash house from the Arab days. Many of the streets end as staircases that descend to the old harbour, where a stone wharf juts into the sea and fishermen still pull their boats up to a pebble beach backed by little houses. What to many visitors is Cefalù's greatest attraction stretches to the south of the old harbour — a long sandy beach that is one of the finest strands in Sicily.

Into the Madonie

South of Cefalù rise the Madonie mountains, a wild landscape of woods, rocks and upland pastures. Every so often the winding roads come to the gates of a pretty hilltown. **Castelbuono**, about 14km (9 miles) south of Cefalù on route 286, climbs

> If a custodian opens a closed church or oratorio for you, show your gratitude with a small tip.

the flanks of the enfolding hills, and its airy piazzas, usually backed by a church or two, afford some lovely views over the mountains. **Petralia Soprana**, 30km (19 miles) further into the mountains, is one of the most beautiful towns in Sicily; it commands a hilltop, and stone palaces and churches line its medieval streets. **Polizzi Generosa**, 15km (9 miles) beyond, is at the head of a green valley and has 76 churches within its walls; the Chiesa Madre is the most opulent, and is decorated with several sculptures by Domenico Gagini. The beautiful landscapes that stretch for miles around these towns are preserved as the **Parco Regionale delle Madonie** and can be traversed on a network of trails.

☞ Tindari

Like so many Greek settlements in Sicily, Tindari is beautifully situated on a headland with sweeping views across the sea to the Aeolian Islands. This view can best be appreciated from the top of the **amphitheatre**. It was built by the Greeks but outfitted for gladiatorial spectacles by the Romans, who conquered the town in 254 BC, barely 150 years after it was founded. A number of Roman houses also still stand, and several retain their colourful mosaic flooring. Tindari, which is about 120km (72 miles) east of Cefalù, is also famous for its **Madonna Nera** (Black Madonna), a Byzantine statue that is much venerated for its miraculous powers. The statue is housed in a huge church erected to accommodate the crowds that make a pilgrimage here, especially on 8 September, her feast day.

The Aeolian Islands (Isole Eolie)

These nine islands and islets off the northeast coast take their name from Aeolus, god of the winds, and it's easy to see why

A lone sailboat plies the wind and seas between the breathtaking Aeolian Islands.

Visitors to Vulcano enjoy a therapeutic soak in one of the island's thermal mud baths.

when a winter gale howls around their peaks. An even more apparent association is with Vulcan, who allegedly had his forge here; the islands' black beaches are telltale signs of millennia of volcanic activity. In fact, fiery eruptions are a daily occurrence on one of the islands, Strómboli, and occur less frequently on the aptly named Vulcano.

Although the islands are small, quiet and best known for such simple pleasures as swimming, hiking and soaking in mud baths, they played an important role in the affairs of the Mediterranean world. Ancient Greeks settled the islands and used them as a base for pirate raids; Carthage launched attacks from them during the Punic Wars; the Romans prized their obsidian (volcanic glass that can be honed to a fine cutting edge); and marauders continued to invade well into the Middle Ages. Today's hordes invade in force in summer months but leave the islanders to themselves at other times. The islands are most easily reached by boat and hydrofoil from Milazzo, a port 150km (90 miles) east of Cefalù.

Vulcano and Lìpari

Vulcano is the island closest to the Sicilian mainland, though Lìpari, just across the narrow Bocche di Vulcano, is the largest and the busiest. Vulcano's steaming volcano supplies the island with its most popular activities: soaking in *fanghi*, thermal mud baths that are said to cure skin disorders and arthritis, and hiking through a lunar landscape to view the crater that is the source of the sulfurous smell that hangs over the main town, Porto di Levante.

On **Lìpari**, the Museo Archeologico displays finds from the islands' long history, including tools and pottery left behind by Neolithic inhabitants; the museum is famous for its terracotta Greek theatre masks and figurines of dancers and actors, the world's largest such collection. Most visitors come to enjoy the island's beaches, many of which are covered in pumice and as a result are white, a curiosity in these parts.

Strómboli

Though Strómboli is small and only sparsely inhabited, it's ever-active volcano has ensured that it is the most famous of the islands. Every 20 minutes or so, the volcanic crater hurls glowing multi-coloured chunks of lava into the sky and down a cliff called the Sciara del

Sulphur vents on Vulcano lend a distinctive odour to the Aeolian air.

Fuoco into the sea, where they hiss and steam. You can witness this spectacle at close range from the rim of the crater; a guided ascent is one of the island's most popular activities and is most rewarding at night. Among the other small islands, **Panaréa** is where rich Italians have sumer homes while **Filicudi** and **Alicudi** are prized for their quiet.

Messina

This busy port town, 200km (124 miles) east of Cefalù, is within sight of mainland Italy across the Strait of Messina. This is often the first place visitors set foot on Sicily; boats ferrying cars and trains across the strait pull in and out of the harbour around the clock. The town's modern appearance and wide boulevards are the outcome of extensive rebuilding after earthquakes (the last one, in 1908, killed 85,000 residents — two-thirds of the population) and massive World War II bombings.

While most visitors hurry on to more atmospheric places, Messina amply rewards a short visit. The duomo at the centre of town is a felicitous and determined reconstruction of the church that Roger II erected in the 12th century. The 1908 earthquake levelled the church, and it was rebuilt in the 1920s. When a 1943 firebombing laid waste to these efforts, the city built the church once again. Some of the sculpture

> Take the receipt: By law, businesses are obligated to issue them, and customers to leave the premises with one.

and mosaic work is original, but much of the church, including the campanile, is a faithful copy. From the heights of the campanile comes a quarter-hourly chime accompanied by a theatrical show of revolving planets, goddesses and beasts; one of them, the town's symbolic lion, roars at noon. The 16th-century **Fontana di Orione** in front of the Duomo has miraculously escaped the ravages that have befallen Messina, and so has the simple, 12th-century church of the **Annunziata dei Catalani**.

Via Garibaldi and its continuation, Via della Libertà, lead north about 2km (1½ miles) through the centre of town to the **Museo Regionale**. This is Sicily's finest art collection, and several works by Antonello da Messina, Sicily's Renaissance master, are here, including his *St Gregory* polyptych. Two of the most stunning works in the museum are by Caravaggio, the *Adoration of the Shepherds* and the *Resurrection of Lazarus*.

THE EASTERN COAST

Sicily's two other large cities, Siracusa and Catania, are on the eastern coast, and so is its most popular resort, Taormina. Remains of Roman and Greek settlements are copious, and many inland towns are built in the style of the Sicilian Baroque. Above all these places looms the fiery peak of Mount Etna, adding quite a bit of drama to the fascinating surroundings.

Taormina

Sicily's most famous resort clings to a hillside high above the sea and, is surrounded by luxurious tropical gardens that bloom year round, with Mount Etna as a backdrop. Taormina also retains the charm of a small, medieval hilltown. Pastel-coloured palaces and churches and a magnificent Greek Theatre are tucked away on narrow, often stepped streets. These charms are not current news — D. H. Lawrence took such a shine to Taormina that he stayed three years, from 1920 to 1923. Taormina is especially popular with vacationers in July and August.

> When riding a bus in Palermo or other Sicilian towns and cities, be sure to stamp your ticket in the machine near the entrance when you get on; you can be fined if you don't.

The main activity in Taormina is strolling the length of its main street, Corso Umberto. Just inside Porta Catania, at the western edge of town, the Corso comes to the Piazza del

Duomo, where the crenellated, fortress-like **cathedral** backs a splashing fountain. After tunneling through the **Torre dell'Orologio**, a 12th-century clock tower, the Corso emerges into the airy **Piazza IX Aprile**, filled with café tables and open on one side to views of the sea and Mount Etna. Many 15th-century palazzi line the Corso; one of them, the Palazzo Carvavia in the Piazza Vittorio Emanuelle, houses the tourist office, and this arrangement makes it possible to catch a glimpse of its ornamentation of black and white lava, the great hall where the Sicilian parliament met in 1410, and the elegant staircase in the courtyard.

Traversing Taormina's main street might be even easier with matching scooters.

The Teatro Greco and Giardino Pubblico

From Piazza Vittorio Emanuelle, the Via Teatro Greco leads to Taormina's beautiful **Greek Theatre**. Though the Romans more or less rebuilt the structure, it is typically Greek in its splendid location, carved into the hillside in such a way that Mount Etna and the sea provide a permanent backdrop. As no less an observer than Goethe once exhaled into his diaries, 'Never did any audience, in any theatre, have before it such a spectacle.' The acoustics are excellent, and the theatre still hosts a summer arts festival.

Via Bagnoli Croce leads downhill off the Corso to the **Giardino Pubblico**, where stands of cypress and cedar frame views of the sea. From the top of the town, a steep path climbs uphill to the ruins of the medieval castello and even higher to the little mountaintop village of Castel Mola. Sooner or later you will want to descend, via funicular if you do not have transportation, to the coast beneath Taormina. The adjoining towns of Mazzarò and Giardini-Naxos provide one long stretch of beach and seaside attractions.

 ## Mount Etna

Europe's largest and most active volcano soars 3,300m (10,000ft) above the Sicilian coast. The fiery mountain has long fascinated residents of Sicily and visitors to the island. Pindar and Pluto wrote about it, Empedocles jumped into its gaseous crater, D. H. Lawrence and legions of other noted observers have waxed poetic about it.

Sicilians keep a close eye on the volcano for good reason: Molten lava flowed through Catania in 1669 and regularly plunges down the mountain towards the towns on its flanks. Eruptions in the summer of 2001 were especially violent, wreaking substantial damage on the roads and mountain cable car and raining ash down on Catania and the rest of the eastern coast. When the volcano is erupting, admirers are allowed to venture no further than Randazzo, Nicolosi and other pleasant towns and resorts in the green foothills; many can be reached on the **Circumetnea** railway, which leaves from Catania and skirts the mountain's lower flanks. Conditions permitting, **Rifugio Sapienza** is the base

> Need to make a call? You'll need a *scheda*, also called a *carta telefonica*. It's a telephone card that's used in public phones and can be purchased at bars, *tabacchi*, and newsstands.

Taormina still hosts a popular summer arts festival at its Greek theatre dramatically situated on the hillside.

from which to make an ascent to the summit on foot or by cable car and Jeep *(see page 87)*.

Catania

Sicily's second largest city, 38km (24 miles) down the coast from Taormina, is grim and industrial in parts, sorely neglected and crime-ridden in others. While the island has more readily appealing places in which to spend time, Catania's lively old centre is fascinating and filled with ancient and Baroque monuments. Many are concentrated on and around Piazza Duomo.

Piazza Duomo

This elegant square is near the port and at the southern end of the Via Etnea. The wide boulevard, Catania's main shopping street, makes a straight run through the city towards the looming, snow-capped volcano, only 20km (12 miles) away. The square and the **Duomo** are the work of Giovanni Battista Vaccarini, who came to Catania in 1730 to rebuild the city from the rubble to which it was reduced in a 1669 lava flow and a 1693 earthquake. Vaccarini's elegant assemblage surrounds the **Fontana dell'Elefante** (Elephant Fountain), crafted like most of Catania's monuments from black lava. Water cascades around a pachyderm with an Egyptian obelisk on its back, creating a pleasing effect that Napoleon copied in several of the monuments he commissioned in Paris.

The **Duomo**'s medieval apses, built of lava, are all that survived the earthquake, and they now lie behind a Baroque façade into which Vaccarini set several columns purloined from Catania's Roman ruins. Vincenzo Bellini, the composer of *Norma* and some of the other most popular operas of the early 19th-century, is buried in the church, as is Saint Agatha, the city's patron. Agatha is a venerated presence in Catania, and has even influenced the city's famous pastries, *seni di vergine* — they are shaped like her breasts, which were mutilated when she was

martyred. (Catania honours Bellini with *spaghetti alla Norma*, named for his famous heroine.) A Roman sarcophagus in the **Cappella della Madonna** contains the mortal remains of Frederick II, Frederick III and Louis, the Aragonese kings who ruled Sicily through the war and plague-ridden 14th century.

Catania's fish, vegetable and fruit market fills the

The Fontana dell'Elefante, crafted from black lava, is a symbol of Catania.

streets to the west of the piazza; to reach the warren of stalls, step through the Porta Uzeda. This lively commerce transpires in the shadows of **Castello Ursino**, the grim fortress from which Frederick II extended a firm hand over his Sicilian kingdom. Frederick built his castle on the seashore, but molten lava from the 1669 eruption landlocked the structure. The cavernous interior houses the eclectic holdings of the **Museo Civico**, recently restored and ranging far and wide, from archaeological finds to Baroque statuary to 19th-century prints.

Piazza Mazzini and Via dei Crociferi

From the gardens in front of the castle it is a short walk up Via Auteri to Piazza Mazzini, surrounded by arcades crafted from 32 columns salvaged from a Roman basilica. More Roman remains rise just to the west: a remarkably intact theatre from the 2nd century BC and a small Odeon used for recitations and rehearsals. Vincenzo Bellini was born in the adjoining Piazza San Francisco, and the composer's house is now the **Museo Belliniano**, filled with his original scores and other memorabilia. A nearby house and museum, just off Corso Vittorio Emanuele on Via Santa Anna, commemorates another noted Catania native, the 19th-century novelist and short story writer Giovanni Verga. Although Verga is little read outside of Italy, his stark depictions of everyday life in Sicily have earned him the reputation as one of the great Italian masters of fiction.

Piazza San Francisco is at the foot of the **Via Crociferi**, lined with Baroque, 18th-century structures. Among them are several churches, of which **San Benedetto** and **San Giuliano** have the most elaborate façades. A few blocks west of San Giuliano, at the end of Via Gesuti, is crescent-shaped **Piazza Dante**. Though the square still manages to conjure the grandeur of days gone by, it is neglected and rather forlorn. The weed-covered façade of the church of **San Nicolò** heightens this sad effect; though the church was never completed, it is the largest in Sicily, and its hulking, massive appearance is rendered all the less appealing by eight ugly columns. Adjoining the church is a massive Benedictine monastery, also in a derelict state.

At the northern end of Via Crociferi, on busy Piazza Stesicoro, looms the hulking **Teatro Romano**. Saint Agatha was thrown to the lions here in 252, before what may have been a sizeable audience — the vast amphitheatre seats 16,000 spectators. Looking up Via Etnea from the front of the theatre, it is easy to comprehend the power of a local legend that claims the citizens of Catania once stopped a lava flow from the nearby mountain by waving the saint's veil in front of it. If Etna is rumbling and spewing during your visit, you may well wish you were equipped with similar protection.

Inland to Enna and Piazza Armerina

Enna, 85km (52 miles) west of Catania on autostrada A 19, is the highest city in Sicily, lying about 900m (3,000ft) above a vast plain that once supplied the Greeks and Romans with wheat. This is not, however, Sicily's most cheerful city, surrounded as it often is by mist and huddled beneath a dark fortress erected by Frederick of Swabia in the 14th century.

On a clear day the views are splendid, and the best places to enjoy them are the central square, Piazza Crispi, or better yet, the Torre Pisana, one of six towers rising above the fortress. On the plains below, wheat fields stretch for miles across the centre of the island. Amid them glimmers **Lago di Pergusa**, the lake where Pluto is said to have abducted Persephone, daughter of Zeus and goddess of fertility, and carried her off to Hades; the wheat died in Persephone's absence, but the earth bloomed anew when Pluto released her.

Piazza Armerina

Most travellers pass through Piazza Armerina, a pleasant hilltown surrounded by forests and fields, on their way to the Roman villa at nearby Casale. The town, 35km (23 miles) south of Enna, warrants a short visit in its own right, too. The 17th-century duomo tops the town, and from the piazza in front the streets wind down the hillside past other churches and palaces to the palm-shaded Piazza Garibaldi.

The Villa Romana at Casale

The Villa Romana is 5km (3 miles) southwest of Piazza Armerina, outside the little hamlet of Casale. Co-emperor Maximillian, who ruled the waning Roman Empire with Diocletian, is thought to have built this elaborate hunting lodge in the 4th century. Later, the villa was abandoned and was eventually buried by landslides and it wasn't completely unearthed until fifty years ago. The many layers of mud that lay atop the ruins for centuries have proved to be a blessing, as they helped preserve the exquisite mosaics with which the villa is floored. Craftsmen from North Africa laid the colourful tiles, filling room after room with hunting scenes, a bestiary of

The old town of Enna. Sicily's highest city is a cool refuge in summer.

Inspecting mosaics of hunting scenes at the Villa Romana.

exotic animals from the far corners of the empire, mythical heroes, chariot races and snippets of everyday life, such as a family preparing to relax in the baths.

The villa's most famous mosaic scenario is the one depicting ten girls, clad in bikinis, competing in a gymnastics competition. Perhaps the most enchanting mosaics, though, are those that decorate the children's quarters; they show young nobles riding chariots pulled by birds, being chased by hares and otherwise engaging in light-hearted play.

Caltagirone

Citizens of this small town 35km (21 miles) southeast of Piazza Armerina have been making ceramics for centuries. They show off their skill on every available surface: Bridges, the 142 steps of La Scala (which climbs one of the town's three hills), the interiors of churches and the façades of houses are tiled with the town's distinctive blue-and-yellow ceramics.

Caltagirone would be attractive even without this adornment, since its old town is filled with Sicilian Baroque and Art Nouveau buildings; the church of **San Francesco d'Assisi** is an especially attractive example of the Sicilian Baroque. The **Museo Regionale della Ceramica** displays work from Caltagirone and elsewhere in Sicily, and the famous local product is for sale in workshops throughout the old town.

Siracusa (Syracuse)

What may well be Sicily's most enticing city is actually three places: the vast Greek and Roman city that played such a prominent role in the ancient world; the island of Ortygia (now Ortigia), where the narrow streets are lined with classical monuments and intricately Baroque churches and palaces; and a ramshackle yet pleasant modern town of broad avenues and sunny seaside promenades. A walk almost anywhere in Siracusa, which is 59km (37 miles) south of Catania, brings you to a remarkable structure or two.

The remains of ancient Syracuse litter every corner of the city, but many are concentrated on the mainland in the **Parco Archeologico**, on the western edge of the modern city at the end of Corso Gelone. Looking at these monuments, it is easy to appreciate the power Siracusa once wielded. Corinthians colonised Siracusa in the 8th century BC, settling on the island of Ortygia. Soon they set their eyes on the rest of Sicily and much of the Mediterranean world, defeating the Carthaginian and Etruscan fleets and eventually, in the so-called Great Expedition of 413 BC, the forces Athens sent to quell the ambitious Siracusans. Under such powerful and often tyrannical rulers as Hieron I and Dionysius the Elder, the city thrived and welcomed Pindar, Aeschylus, Plato and other great minds of the Hellenistic world.

The Romans, against whom Sircacusa fought in the Second Punic War, finally subdued the city in 211BC. Though Siracusa never again regained its power, natural harbours ensured the city would remain an important trading post. Early Christianity, bolstered by a visit from Saint Paul, flourished in Siracusa, and extensive catacombs beneath the city served as both tombs and churches. Although the city was briefly the capital of the Byzantine Empire, from 663 to 668, it more or less languished through successive conquests by Arabs, Normans and Bourbons. It flowered briefly again in the early 18th century, when much of Ortigia was rebuilt in the excessive style of the Baroque.

The Parco Archeologico

Much of ancient Siracusa was built of limestone that slaves, captured in the city's numerous sea battles, dug out of quarries called the **Latomie**. Now overgrown with tropical foliage that lends a garden-like aspect to the archaeological park, the Latomie were also used as prisons. The cavern dubbed **Orecchio di Dionisio**, Ear of Dionysius, seems to have been especially well suited to this purpose; legend has it the tyrant made use of the unusual acoustics, which allowed him to stand at the entrance and overhear anything a prisoner or guard within might whisper. The dampness of the adjoining **Grotta dei Cordari** provided ideal conditions for ropemakers, rendering the strands more pliant; the ropes fashioned here thousands of years ago have left deep indentations in the rocks.

Just beyond the Ear of Dionysius is the **Teatro Greco**, one of the largest Greek theatres in the ancient world. Aeschylus wrote works to be performed on its stage. Of the original 59 rows of seats, 42 still remain and are filled during the summer months for popular performances of some of the ancient Greek dramas. The **Anfiteatro Romano** served less refined tastes; built in the 3rd century AD, it staged circuses and gladiatorial events. Hieron II, who ruled all of Sicily from Siracusa throughout much of the 3rd century BC, commissioned his eponymous **Ara di Ierone II**. The largest sacrificial altar in the Greek world was 200m (660ft) long and could accommodate 450 bulls at a time.

Basilica di San Giovanni and the Catacombs

Orecchio di Dionisio graces the grounds of Siracusa's archaeological park.

Other remnants of ancient Siracusa are scattered about the city, often neglected and choked by weeds. The old agora and Ginnasio Romano, a small theatre, are tucked away in patches of greenery (often overlooked) in the shabby southern precincts of the modern city, near the port and train station. A much-visited site is the city's oldest church, the **Basilica di San Giovanni**, just north of Via Teócrito. Though the church has been a roofless ruin since the earthquake of 1693, it is possible to find the spot where Saint Paul delivered a sermon and the pillar to which Saint Marcian, the first bishop of Siracusa, was tied and flogged to death in 254. Steps descend to the **catacombs**, part of a vast network of caverns that often follows the paths of subterranean Greek aqueducts. They provided a place of refuge for Christians during times of Roman persecution. Christian burial was forbidden under Roman law, so the passageways also served as tombs; it is believed that more than 20,000 early Christians are buried beneath San Giovanni.

The Museo Archeologico

Many of the finds from ancient Siracusa are displayed in the **Museo Archeologico Regionale Paolo Orsi**, just south of San Giovanni on Via Teócrito. This is one of the most exten-

sive archaeological collections in Europe and ranges far beyond Siracusa into the rest of the Mediterranean world. The prize of the collection, though, is from Siracusa: a headless Venus Anadiomene, modestly covering her nudity as she emerges from the water. Among the votive statuettes, burial urns and torsos are tools and skeletons of the Stone and Bronze Age peoples who inhabited this corner of Sicily long before the Greeks arrived.

Tempio di Apollo, one of many ancient wonders on the island of Ortigia.

The small **Museo del Papiro** next door displays ancient papyrus manuscripts and other artifacts. Ancient Siracusans are believed to have brought the plant back from their exploits in North Africa, and you may notice clumps of it in the city's gardens — the only place in Europe it grows.

Ortigia

This small island, ancient Ortigia, is separated from the mainland by a narrow channel, and crammed with the remnants of more than 2,500 years of history.

The **Tempio di Apollo** is at the end of Ponte Nuovo. A few broken columns and marble fragments are all that remains of the structure, which dates from 565BC and is thought to be the oldest Doric temple in Sicily. The Corso Matteoti leads from the temple to Piazza Archimede, named for the Greek

> On some of the more remote islands where lodging is in private homes, look for signs that say *'Camere Libre'* (Rooms Available).

mathematician and inventor who was a 3rd-century BC resident of the city. The Piazza Duomo, just south along the Via Roma, is one of the most attractive squares in Italy, providing an appropriate setting for the cathedral and some of the island's grandest palaces.

The **Duomo** is a blend of architectural styles from Siracusa's long history. It incorporates the body of a temple of Athena the Siracusans built in thanksgiving for their victory over the Carthaginians at Himera in the 6th century BC; you can see 12 columns from the temple, one of the most splendidly decorated in the ancient world is located in the north wall. The church took on Byzantine elements when it became the first Christian cathedral of Siracusa in 640AD, a Norman façade that was replaced when it collapsed in the earthquake of 1693 and the Baroque elements that are much in evidence today. The interior is quite sparse, but houses a number of statues by the Gagini, the illustrious clan of Baroque sculptors, and a fine painting of Saint Zosimus by Antonello da Messina.

Fonte Aretusa and Galleria Regionale

The western shore of Ortigia, just a few steps in front of Piazza Duomo, is one long seaside esplanade, the Foro Italico. This is where Siracusans come for an evening *passeggiata*, accompanied by a view of the setting sun. Lord Nelson docked here, beside the **Fonte Aretusa**, to take on fresh water en route to the Battle of the Nile. He drew from a renowned source: the fountain was famous throughout the ancient world as the metamorphosed nymph Arethusa. Fleeing the unwanted attentions of the river god Alpheus, she called on the goddess Artemis for help. Artemis turned her into a spring, and she flowed beneath the Mediterranean and emerged here — to no avail, since Alpheus followed her and forever mingles his waters with hers. The fountain continues to gush into a pool overgrown with papyrus.

The Via Capodieci leads inland again to a handsome group of palaces. One of them, the 13th to 15th century **Palazzo Bellomo**, houses the **Galleria Regionale**, the regional art gallery. Two fine paintings grace the salons of the upper floor, a greatly restored *Annunciation* by Antonello da Messina and *Burial of St Lucy* by Caravaggio; the Caravaggio was moved here for safe keeping from the church of Santa Lucia up the street. One of the best ways to enjoy Ortigia is to amble through its narrow streets and dusty piazzas at your leisure, a walk that rewards you with quiet scenes of Sicilian life.

Inland from Siracusa

The rocky plains and scrubby mountains that lie inland from Siracusa are littered with more ancient remains; it was here, too, that the Sicilian Baroque flowered in several small towns.

Castello Eurialo

This military complex on the plains 8km (5 miles) west of Siracusa, commemorates the art of ancient warfare. Dionysius the Elder built a massive fort here, and later modifications engineered by Archimedes have ensured the defences are the largest and most intricate fortifications to survive from the ancient Greek world. A network of walls, surrounded by three defensive trenches, once extended for 30km (18 miles) — encircling all of ancient Siracusa. Many parts of the walls

remain, as do the keep, towers from which soldiers manned catapults and underground escape routes. Elaborate as the defences were, history would prove that they were built in vain — Siracusa eventually surrendered without a fight to the Roman legions.

Palazzolo Acrèide

Palazzolo Acrèide, 45km (28 miles) west of Siracusa,

The Piazza Duomo, like the rest of Ortigia, is saturated in colourful history.

was an early colony of ancient Siracusa, founded as **Akrai** in the 7th century BC. It's hard to get a sense of Akrai's one-time glory in the clutter of its ruins, but the lovely, semicircular **Teatro Greco** is well preserved. Among the ruins are remnants of early devotion: Early Christians cut their catacombs into the quarries that supplied stone for the city, and members of a 3rd-century BC cult carved **Santoni**, with life-size images of the fertility goddess Cybele, into a nearby rock face.

The pleasant 'new' town is filled with Baroque palaces and churches, and its **Casa-Museo di Antonio Uccello** displays an intriguing collection of tools, furniture and other objects that were once mainstays of rural Sicilian life. The Baroque ornamentation of Palazzolo Acrèide is a preview of the town called Noto, just 6km (4 miles) down the road.

Noto

When an earthquake levelled Noto on 11 January 1693, architects immediately set to work rebuilding the town. The Sicilian Baroque, a flamboyantly ornamental architectural style, was in full flower, and Noto was a blank canvas on which to show it off. Corso Vittorio Emanuele and the central Piazza del Municipo are fantasies of curving staircases, elaborate balconies and porticos, and richly detailed façades.

Looking at the **Duomo** atop a dramatic staircase and the heavily colonnaded **Municipio**, it's hard to believe Noto is built of solid stone. In truth, it's not — the architects used soft local stone, and as a result much of Noto, like the collapsed cathedral dome, is in urgent need of repair. Many of the buildings are shrouded in scaffolding and shored up with timbers. Like all fantasies, Noto is quite fragile.

Viewing Ragusa Ibla from Largo Santa Maria

Ragusa

Ragusa, 50km (30 miles) west of Noto, is another Baroque town — at least half of one, since the older Baroque section, Ragusa Ibla, is separated from the newer, more ordinary Ragusa Superiore by a deep gorge. A flight of 242 steps climbs up and down the hillsides into the quiet streets and piazzas of **Ragusa Ibla**; the church of Santa Maria delle Scale (Saint Mary of the Steps) is a welcome spot to rest midway and enjoy a stunning view over the ochre-coloured town. At the highest point of Ragusa Ibla is the Piazza Duomo and Basilico di San Giorgio. Palm trees, a curving staircase leading up to the church and a façade of columns and balconies create a masterfully Baroque scene.

THE SOUTHERN COAST

Two of the ancient world's greatest cities are next to the sea on the southern coast of Sicily, and Arab colonists have left their mark as well.

Agrigento

The poet Pindar described the city the Greeks knew as Akragas as the 'fairest of mortal cities'. You probably won't disagree with the sentiment as you look upon the dramatic vestiges of the ancient city, where a row of temples follows a ridge above the sea and a valley littered with ruins set among olive trees.

Unfortunately, the modern world intrudes upon this idyllic scene rather rudely. Modern buildings, constructed illegally, encroach upon the ruins. Workaday Agrigento, which occupies a hillside above the ancient city, is undistinguished, hastily put up in the 1960s after overbuilding triggered a catastrophic mudslide. What brings visitors to Agrigento, which is on the centre of the southern coast about 240km (149 miles) west of Siracusa, are the ruins of the ancient city spread across the so-called Valle dei Templi (Valley of the Temples).

Valley of the Temples

The best way to enjoy ancient Agrigento is to follow the **Strada Panoramica** and Via dei Templi through the ruins of what was the wealthiest Greek city in Sicily. Settlers from Rhodes and Gela in 582BC, Agrigento provided a good harbour and fertile soil and soon flourished — first under the tyrannical Phalaris, a member of a bull cult who allegedly burned his enemies alive in a bronze bull, then under Theron, who by the early 5th century BC had defeated the Carthaginians and extended the power of Akragas over much of the Mediterranean.

The city became known for its wealth and as a flourishing capital of 200,000 people who promoted the arts, philosophy and chariot racing. Empedocles, a native, developed the theory of the four elements (Earth, Air, Wind and Fire) and died when he dove into the crater of Mount Etna to investigate his premises; the philosopher commented, 'The city's citizens enjoy life as they would die tomorrow, but they build palaces as if to live forever.' This prosperity, however, was short lived. Carthage sacked the city in 406BC, and Rome invaded in 210BC.

The first temple you come to on a walk south through the valley is the **Tempio di Giuonen (Juno)**, built by the Greeks in 460BC, and restored by the Romans after the handsome structure was destroyed by the Carthaginians; the stones are still scorched from the fires the invaders set. Earthquakes have also taken their toll, though a sacrificial altar and 25 of the 34 original columns have been set back in place.

The **Tempio della Concordia**, built around 450BC, is the best preserved temple at Agrigento (largely because it was converted to a Christian church in the 6th century), and one of the finest Doric temples of the ancient world. The stucco that once covered the temple has long since worn away, exposing warm, golden stone that, in combination with the 34 original columns that still surround it, lends a proud and solid appearance.

The oldest temple at Agrigento is the **Tempio di Ercole (Hercules)**, dating from the 6th century BC and now a romantic jumble of ruins from which nine of its original columns still emerge.

In Agrigento, ancient ruins stand in a valley beneath the new city.

Valley of the Temples — Agrigento was once renowned as the wealthiest Greek city in Sicily.

A statue of Hercules and a fresco depicting the young god grappling with serpents once graced the temple, but these have long since vanished.

Much of the rest of the valley is strewn with the rubble of other temples and monuments. The stony remains of the **Tempio di Giove Olimpico (Jove)** are copious enough to suggest that this was indeed the largest Doric temple ever built. Enormous *telamones* (columns fashioned in the shape of male figures) once supported the massive structure, and a reproduction of one of them, the so-called Gigante, lies on the ground among the ancient debris.

The Museo Archeologico and the Roman City

The original Gigante is now in the **Museo Archeologico Regionale**, surrounded by other finds from the city and the surrounding province. Delicate vases, terracotta figurines and an alabaster sarcophagus designed for a young boy and etched with scenes from his childhood provide an evocative glimpse into life in the ancient city. Next to the museum spread the remains of the settlement that the Romans established when they took Agrigento permanently in 210BC. Many of the houses they constructed on the Greek streets still stand, and their mosaic flooring is remarkably intact.

At the eastern edge of the valley, alongside the fortifications with which the Greeks surrounded the city, is the church of **San Biagio**. The Normans built this small, simple structure on the site of a temple dedicated to Demeter and Persephone. Below the church, and reached by a steep staircase carved into the cliff, is the **Santuario di Demetra**. Hundreds of votive objects and an elaborate system of terracotta pipes and cisterns suggest the sanctuary's two caverns may have been used by a cult during the earliest days of Agrigento.

Modern Agrigento

The modern city also bears some traces of Agrigento's ancient inhabitants: **Santa Maria dei Greci**, a small basilica rising above the stepped streets of the medieval quarter, is built of antique materials on the site of a temple to Athena; several columns are imbedded in the walls of the church. Luigi Pirandello, Agrigento's acclaimed 20th-century novelist and dramatist, was born in the seaside suburb of **Caos**. His birthplace, the **Casa Natale di Luigi Pirandello**, is now a museum, and his ashes are buried beneath a lone pine tree in the garden.

Sciacca

This unspoiled seaside town 65km (41 miles) northwest of Agrigento is still engaged in the pursuits that have occupied its citizens for millennia: fishing in the waters between Sicily and Africa and ministering to patrons of its thermal spa.

Residents of ancient Selunis, just down the coast, came here to soak in the warm, mineral-rich waters that emerge from deep beneath nearby Monte San Calogero, and the thermal station still provides a full regimen of treatments. The town that climbs the hillside above the busy fishing port is flat-roofed and whitewashed, a legacy of many years of Arab habitation. Among the later structures rising above the warren of little stepped streets are the 17th-century Duomo and the simpler, 12th-century church of **San Nicolò La Latina**.

Caltabellotta, a small town that clings to three rocky promontories high in the mountains above Sciacca, played an important role in Sicilian history. In its now-ruined castle, Charles of Valois and Frederick of Aragon signed the treaty that ended the 13th-century revolt against French rule known as the War of the Vespers.

The ruined temples of Selinunte represent an ancient Greek city that was never fully realised.

Selinunte

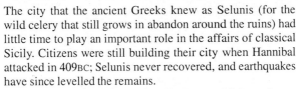

The city that the ancient Greeks knew as Selunis (for the wild celery that still grows in abandon around the ruins) had little time to play an important role in the affairs of classical Sicily. Citizens were still building their city when Hannibal attacked in 409BC; Selunis never recovered, and earthquakes have since levelled the remains.

Even so, Selinunte, 45km (27 miles) west of Sciacca, is one of the most evocative ancient sites in the Mediterranean, with ruined temples and monuments that now stand in lonely fields next to the sea. Three of the temples have been partially restored. They are designated by letter rather than name; to whom they were dedicated remains uncertain. **Temple E** is closest to the sea, and its massive columns have been set upright. **Temple G** was one of the largest Doric structures in Greek Sicily, though it was never completed; unfinished column blocks lie among its rubble. **Temple C** stands at the highest point of the acropolis and has provided the archaeological museum in Palermo with some of its greatest treasures — the metopes, or decorative friezes, that were once set atop its columns. The new settlement, **Marinella di Selinunte**, is a quiet fishing port and resort with a long, sandy beach.

THE WEST COAST

Western Sicily was settled by Phoenicians, Greeks, Romans, Arabs, and the great European powers of the Middle Ages, and their presence is still much in evidence.

Marsala

This sleepy city 70km (43 miles) north and west of Selinunte has a long and raucous past. The Phoenicians settled here in the 8th century BC, abandoned the city when they made the island of **Mozia** their stronghold, and came back when the Siracusans routed them in 397BC. After a ten-year siege, the Romans took the city in 241BC. Lilybaeum, as the city was then called, become the seat of the Roman governor of Sicily; by the time Caesar arrived on his way to Africa in 47BC, Cicero had dubbed Lilybaeum a *civitas splendidissima*.

The port also proved to be a convenient gateway for the Arabs who overran Sicily in the 9th century; they called it 'the harbour of Allah', or *Marsala Allah*. On 11 May 1860, the port of Marsala welcomed Garibaldi and the Thousand, the red-shirted freedom fighters who freed Sicily from Bourbon rule to unite Italy as a republic.

Capo Boéo

Marsala bears its past glories with modesty. Of the ancient city, little remains but fragments of the Roman walls, some baths and a 3rd-century villa that's decorated with mosaics of hunting scenes and the four seasons; these are concentrated in the archaeological zone on a promontory at the western edge of the city known as **Capo Boéo**, which also happens to be the westernmost point in Sicily.

The nearby **Museo Archeologico** displays more Roman finds, including some colourful wall paintings and Phoenician ceramics. Most interesting, though, is a **Phoenician warship** that the Romans probably sank in the First Punic War. Discovered in 1971 on the seabed just north of Marsala, the boat is one of the few warships to survive from antiquity and has provided archaeologists with a wealth of information about the arts of ancient warfare. The poop deck and parts of the hull, which was originally 35m (120ft) long, are remarkably intact; just as fascinating are the buttons, needles, corks and everyday objects that were found on board.

The Old Town

The sweet, pleasant scent that pervades the city is that of an elixir that brought Marsala fame and fortune in the 18th century. An Englishman, John Woodhouse, began shipping the local wine back home in 1773, adding a little extra alcohol as a preservative. Simply called Marsala, the wine soon became enormously popular. Wine merchants built stone warehouses along the port from which they still export the sweet wine around the world; one of them, the house of Florio on the Lungomare Mediterraneo, offers tastings.

British warships sent to protect England's interests in the Marsala business proved to be convenient for Garibaldi, who assumed they would also protect him when he made his landing here in 1860. His presence in Marsala is commemorated by the Porta Garibaldi and the Via Garibaldi, which leads north from the port to the **Piazza della Repubblica,** the centre of town. The **Palazzo Comunale** and the **Duomo** face the square. Both have Baroque, 18th-cenutry façades; sculptures by Antonello Gagini decorate the church.

The church is another example of the city's ties to England. It is dedicated to San Tommaso di Canterbury,

Windmills once used for refining salt still dot the landscape near Mozia.

What's most appealing about Trapani, a lively port town since Phoenician times, is its seaside setting.

also known as Saint Thomas Becket, who was murdered by knights of King Henry II when he defended the rights of the church against lay power. A ship carrying columns from Corinth to the saint's city of Canterbury was forced to take shelter at Marsala during a storm. The columns went no further and now line the nave of the duomo; considering this twist of events to be provident, the city made Thomas its patron saint.

In the **Museo degli Arazzi**, behind the duomo, hang eight Flemish tapestries that depict the Capture of Jerusalem. They were a gift from Antonio Lombardo, a 16th-century Marsala native who was the archbishop of Messina and the Sicilian ambassador to Spain; he, in turn, received the sumptuous weavings from the court of Philip II.

☞ Mozia

The Phoenicians colonised the tiny island of San Pantelo in the 8th century BC and built Mozia, one of their three cities on Sicily. They remained until Dionysius, the power-hungry Siracusan, routed them in 397BC.

The Phoenicians went back and forth across the lagoon on a raised road, which now lay submerged beneath the shallow waters. Today's visitors reach the island by the ferry that departs from a landing about 15km (9 miles) north of Marsala or, more in keeping with ancient ways, in one of the rowboats for rent. The mainland near San Pantelo is marshy and parceled into salt pans, and windmills that were once used to refine the salt rise above the flat landscape; one of the mills near the landing, the **Mulino Salina Infersa**, houses a museum devoted to salt extraction.

Joseph Whitaker, from a prosperous family of Marsala wine exporters, bought the island and began to excavate the ruins in 1913. His finds lay scattered across the tiny, almost deserted island: a house with a floor of pebble mosaics, a small dockyard, fortifications and a gate, and a burial ground dedicated to the goddess Tanit and the god Baal Hammon, to whom children were sacrificed. The **Museo Whitaker** displays objects unearthed among the ruins, including the famous *Giovane in Tunica*, an exquisite, 5th-century BC marble statue of a young man in a tunic who may have been a charioteer.

Trapani

This city in the centre of the western coast, 32km (19 miles) north of Marsala, is a workaday place, and much of its business is said to concern Mafia drug trafficking and money laundering. Even so, Trapani has been a lively port town since Phoenician times, and the setting is lovely. The old city is squeezed onto a narrow promontory that juts far into the sea, and the outskirts trail off into salt marshes where windmills catch Mediterranean breezes.

Most visitors hurry through Trapani on their way to **Erice**, the stone town that hovers high above it. It's well worth taking the time, though, to stroll down the Corso Vittorio Emanuele to the **Torre di Ligny**, a Spanish fortress at the end of the promontory. The street is lined with Baroque palaces and churches, and the sea poetically frames the end of the narrow side streets.

The Egadi Islands (Isole Ègadi)

Trapani is the jumping-off point for the three islands in this sparsely populated archipelago; the nearest and largest island, Favignana, is only 25 minutes away by hydrofoil *(see page 124)*.

All of the islands offer fine beaches and good walks across unspoiled landscapes, and each has its own character. **Favignana** is the most populated, though only 3,000 people live on the island and the number is decreasing with the decline of a once thriving tuna industry. Even so, the springtime *la mattanza* is still a major event on the island — in this well-orchestrated spectacle, fishermen net and harpoon hundreds of tuna at a time.

> **Cover up when you leave the beach; Sicilians don't think kindly of visitors who walk through town, even in a resort, in bathing suits.**

On barren **Levanzo**, prehistoric inhabitants of the cave now known as the **Grotta del Genovese** left behind Neolithic paintings and Paleolithic carved drawings, mostly of animals. The images are between 6,000 and 10,000 years old and weren't discovered until 1950. You can reach the caves by boat from the port in Levanzo town, or walk to them along the island's only road and a dirt path; both routes provide views of the **Faraglione**, a rocky spire erupting from the sea.

Marettimo is the most isolated of the islands, and unlike Favignana and Levanzo, is mountainous and verdant and has a rugged coastline that shelters many beach-backed coves. Any resemblance this lovely landscape bears to those described in ancient myth may not be coincidental; it's been suggested that Marettimo is Ithaca, the home to which Odysseus yearned to return.

Pantelleria

This windswept island is closer to North Africa than it is to the rest of Sicily, 110km (66 miles) from Trapani and 70km (42 miles) from Tunisia. Pantelleria can be reached by plane or boat from Trapani and by plane from Palermo and rewards the effort with warm water for swimming off its rocky shores and dramatic volcanic landscapes. The island also provides the opportunity to experience an unusual climatic phenomenon, a constant breeze that gives Pantelleria its name, from the Arabic *bint-al-rian*.

A ferry will take you from Trapani to the Egadi Islands, where you'll find excellent beaches and unspoiled environs.

A good network of buses provides transport to most spots of interest, including the island's few manmade attractions. These include remnants of prehistoric settlers; the most fascinating is **Sesi**, a collection of funeral mounds on the southwest coast in which black volcanic rock is piled into high mounds. More in evidence are the island's distinctive houses, called *dammusi*. Arab colonists introduced these whitewashed cubes, fashioned from volcanic stone, and the islanders continue to build them.

Similarly exotic is the island's black soil, the legacy of its volcanic peak. It is well suited to growing capers and the *zibibbo* grape vines from which some excellent wines are produced; the most unusual is *passito*, a sweet dessert wine. The volcanic presence also accounts for the hot springs that bubble up around the island. Some of the most appealing are at **Scauri**, not far from Sesi, where you can soak in warm natural pools and then jump into the sea.

☛ Erice

Just 10km (6 miles) northeast of Trapani, Erice is a world apart from that city or any place else in the modern world. Isolated on the heights of Monte Erice, the town has always enjoyed a lofty status. The ancient Elymians called the city Eryx and built a temple dedicated to Aphrodite (the Roman Venus), goddess of fertility. Aside from gathering fame throughout the Mediterranean world for its rich decoration, the temple served as a beacon for sailors navigating the trade routes to and from Africa. The Romans restored the temple several times; the Arabs considered the town holy enough to dub it *Gebel-Hamed*, Mohammed's Mountain; and the Norman Count Roger had visions of St Julian while besieging Erice and renamed it Monte San Giuliano. Even Mussolini saw the sanctity of the town and revived its ancient name.

The Normans built their **Castello di Vénere** on the site of the ancient temple, taking advantage of the commanding position at the top of the town. Erice's public gardens now surround the castle, and from them rises the 15th-century **Torretta Pepoli**; both castle and tower are ivy-covered, and the views from the garden terraces, over the plains and sea far below, are expansive — in fact, some keen-eyed observers claim to have seen all the way to Cap Bon in Tunisia.

The rest of the town is mostly medieval and clings precipitously to the shoulder of the summit. Battlements atop the tower of the stone **Chiesa Madre** are evidence of the double duty it did for the armies of Frederick III of Aragon, who used it as a lookout post; the interior of the church is surprisingly light and airy. At the heart of the city is its only square, Piazza Umberto I. The **Museo Civico Cordici** occupies an upper floor of one of the surrounding buildings; in it is a relief of the *Annunciation* by Antonello Gagini, considered to be one of his finest works. Given its medieval quiet and spacious views, Erice is a pleasant place to stop for a few days, and it is within easy reach of most of the sights on the western and southern coasts.

With spectacular views and sense of tranquillity, Erice makes for a great getaway.

Segesta

The Elymians, who lavished such attention on the temple in Erice *(see page 78)*, settled Segesta in the 12th century BC. By the 5th century BC, when Segesta's temple was built, the city had been heavily influenced by the Greeks who had colonised the island. It was busy warring with Selinunte, its neighbour on the southern coast.

The temple and a well-preserved theatre are the only size-able remains of the ancient city, which is still being excavated. Their isolation, in green hills about 30km (18 miles) east of Trapani, lend the site a singular beauty. Both are among the finest monuments of antiquity, and both are set on hills looking over the rolling countryside and the sea.

> If you arrive at a church when a Mass is being said, stay quietly in the rear; better yet, come back at another time.

The **temple** looks as if it were never completed — the columns are not fluted, and there is no *cella*, or sanctuary. Some scholars believe that builders had to lay down their tools and take up arms to ward off a series of attacks from Selinunte, and others suggest that the unusual design was intentional. The **theatre**, meanwhile, has been much used, and still stages classical and contemporary dramas.

Capo San Vito

This mountainous cape at the northwestern tip of Sicily, 40km (25 miles) north of Trapani, has the finest beaches on the island and rugged headlands that are ideal for hiking. In the **Riserva Naturale dello Zingaro**, a nature preserve just to the southeast, paths follow 6km (4 miles) of forested coastline that is etched with lovely coves.

WHAT TO DO

Aside from the extensive remnants of past ages, Sicily provides many other diversions. Many of these activities allow you to enjoy the island's beautiful landscapes of seacoasts and mountains.

SHOPPING

If you are coming to Italy to shop, you are well advised to save your hard-earned money until you reach Rome, Florence, Milan, or one of Italy's other shopping meccas. In Sicily the years of poverty and ongoing high unemployment become apparent in the dearth of chic shops that are so common on the Italian mainland. The best places to shop here are the markets that fill the streets of every city and town.

You are most likely to find what the island offers in the way of high fashion and other worldly goods in Palermo and Taormina. In Palermo, most of the better shops are concentrated around Piazza Verdi and Via della Libertà. In Taormina, the Corso Umberto is lined with fine shops. Catania's Via Etnea, especially between Piazza Stesicoro and Piazza del Duomo, is the main shopping precinct. In Siracusa, the island of Ortigia is becoming more of a sophisticated urban centre all the time, and several clothing and home furnishings shops are opening on and around Piazza Archimede.

There are a few special items to look for as you tour the island.

Antiques. Some of the most distinctive items to show up in antiques shops are pieces of the painted carts (*carretti siciliani*) that were once the mainstay of transport in the countryside. You can occasionally find plaques of wood from the carts covered in bright designs in the antiques shops of Palermo, Erice and Taormina. Another place to look for

Painted models of the pony-drawn Sicilian carts make great gifts.

them is among the stalls of the daily flea market behind the cathedral in Palermo.

Ceramics. The town of Caltagirone, southwest of Catania, has been producing ceramics for centuries — even the 142 steps of its monumental staircase are covered in colourful tiles of local manufacture *(see page 57)*. Workshops around the town continue to make and sell tiles and other ceramics goods. Sciacca, on the southern coast, also makes ceramics and several shops in the old town sell them *(see page 69)*.

Crafts. Erice is known for its hand-loomed cotton rugs, and they are available in several shops in town. In Taormina, several shops sell embroidered linens. Many villagers on the island still weave baskets, and sell them at local markets.

Papyrus. The ancients brought this African plant to Siracusa, and the city is now the only place in Europe where it grows. The Museo del Papiro there demonstrates how the reeds are made into paper and a few craftspeople sell sheets of papyrus as well as boxes and other small objects made from it *(see page 61)*.

Souvenirs. Aside from the glowing replicas of Mount Etna and all manner of items made from black lava – from statues to ashtrays – look for the delightful replicas of the puppets that are the stars of Sicily's popular puppet theaters; the Museo Internazionale delle Marionette in Palermo *(see page 34)* can direct you to craftspeople who make the most authentic replicas of the puppets.

Weekly Markets

Sicilian street markets provide most of the staples of life, and vendors sell clothing, household items, hardware, appliances and an enormous variety of food, including fresh fruit, vegetables, seafood, meat and cheese. In most you'll also come upon stalls selling fast food, such as fried calamari or sandwiches, and in the large, daily markets in bigger cities there are usually several excellent restaurants. Any town of any size in Sicily has a market at least one day a week, usually in the morning.

In Palermo, the two largest markets in the centre of the city

are the *Vucciria*, in a warren of streets near the intersection of Via Roma and Corso Vittorio Emanuele *(see page 30)*, and the *Ballarò*, around Piazza Carmine in the Albergheria quarter *(see page 27)*. Both are held daily except Sunday. There is also a daily flea market in the streets behind the cathedral. In Catania, the market fills the streets between Piazza Duomo and Castello Ursino.

No need to worry about a souvenir shortage, on Monte Pellegrino or anywhere else.

Festivals and Seasonal Events

Sicilians celebrate festivals year round. Some, but certainly not all of them, include:

6 January In Piana degli Albanesi outside of Palermo, costumed citizens join a procession to celebrate Epiphany.

Early February The Valle dei Templi is the setting for the Sagra del Mandorlo in Fiore (Almond Blossom Festival).

3–5 February In Catania, the relics of city patron Santa Agata are paraded through town to the accompaniment of fireworks and a street fair.

February–March Many towns celebrate Carnevale, most notably Sciacca, Cefalù, Taormina, and (with the most lavish parades and other festivities), Acireale, north of Catania.

Holy Week Erice, Noto, Enna, Trapani, Marsala, and many other towns note this solemn religious period with special observations; however, in San Fratello, in the hills above Cefalù, citizens celebrate the Festa dei Giudei (Feast of the Jews) by donning costumes and parading through the streets on Maundy Thursday and Good Friday.

May–June On Favignana in the Egadi Islands, fishing boats head out to sea for *la mattanza,* in which hundreds of tuna are netted and harpooned.

27–29 June Sciacca hosts a big fish fry.

July Caos, outside Agrigento, honors native son Luigi Pirandello with performances of his plays.

10–15 July All of Palermo takes to the streets for a boisterous festival in honor of Santa Rosalia, the city's patron.

21–30 July International festival of cinema, dance and music in Taormina's Greek theatre.

24–25 July Caltagirone illuminates the tiled steps of its magnificent stairway, the Scala, with oil lamps.

First week of August Siracusa hosts its *palio,* in which boats manned by crews from the town's five quarters race around Ortygia island.

13–14 August In Piazza Armerina, the Palio dei Normanni is accompanied by medieval pageantry to celebrate the taking of the town by Count Roger.

15 August (Ferragosta) The resort of Capo d'Orlando, east of Cefalù, celebrates the Feast of the Assumption with a procession of boats; in Messina, plaster giants *(giganti)* and a massive float of Christ surrounded by angels are pulled through town in three days of festivities.

24 August The island of Lipari celebrates the feast of San Bartolomeo with fireworks and a procession around a statue of the saint.

August–September In Cáccamo, which is between Palermo and Cefalù, some 500 citizens dress themselves as luminaries from the town's past during La Castellana, an historical pageant.

4 September The faithful make a pilgrimage up Monte Pellegrino to the Sanctuario di Santa Rosario to commemorate the saint's feast day.

8 September The sanctuary of the Black Madonna in Tindari is a pilgrimage destination.

December Opera seaon begins in Palermo. Taormina celebrates the Christmas season with concerts and puppet shows and kicks off the New Year with a spectacular fireworks display.

13 December Siracusans carry a silver statue of their patron, Santa Lucia, through the streets to commemorate her feast.

In addition to the popular models sold as souvenirs, distinctively painted Sicilian carts come in full sizes too.

SPORTS AND OUTDOOR ACTIVITIES

With its balmy weather and beautiful landscapes, Sicily provides plenty of outdoor activities.

Hiking. Sicily's rugged terrain is well suited to hiking, though there are relatively few established trail networks. An exception is the Madonie mountains, where marked trails ascend the peak of Pizzo Carbonara (1,979 metres, 6,495ft) and crisscross the wooded terrain beneath them; the tourist office in Cefalù can provide information *(see page 127)*. The Riserva Naturale dello Zingaro protects the coast just east of Capo San Vito, and its trails follow the sea (from them you can scramble down to secluded coves) and cut through forest-covered mountainsides. The tourist office in Capo San Vito provides a wealth of information on the reserve *(see page 127)*.

The islands off Sicily also offer many hiking opportunities; in fact, in the absence of roads and cars, the only way to traverse some of them is on foot. This is, for instance, the case on Marettimo in the Egadi islands, where paths take you through beautiful, wild scenery to secluded beaches. In the Aeolians, the remote islands of Filicudi and Alicudi present some excellent terrain for hiking.

Scuba diving and snorkeling. The waters off Ustica, a tiny island 60km (36 miles) north of Palermo, provide the best locale for both activities. A stretch of the coastline is designated as a natural marine reserve, and equipment rentals and dive schools are plentiful. The tourist office in Palermo provides information on the island and its underwater activities.

Skiing. While Sicily will never be an internationally renowned ski resort, its higher peaks have lifts and other facilities. In the Madonie mountains, the main ski resort is the alpine village of Piano Battaglia; the tourist information in Cefalù can provide information *(see page 127)*. On Mount Etna, the village of

Linguaglossa is the main ski center; the tourist office there, Tel. (095) 643094, provides information on lifts and equipment rentals.

Swimming. The beaches at Sicily's famous seaside resorts of Cefalù and Taormina are adequate but crowded, and the same can be said of Mondello, the seaside getaway for Palermo. You'll find more isolation on the beaches on Capo San Vito and, especially, in the adjoining Zingaro nature reserve; in the reserve you may be able to find a secluded cove of your own. Some of the most enjoyable swimming is from the

Four-wheel-drive vehicles will take you in for a closer look at volcanic Mount Etna.

beaches on the islands off Sicily — especially Marettimo in the Egadi Islands and the less-crowded of the Aeolians.

Volcano Viewing. Sicily has two of the few active volcanoes in Europe, Mount Etna on the island's eastern coast and Strómboli in the Aeolian Islands. Conditions permitting, you can begin an ascent to the crater area on Etna from Rifugio Sapienza on foot or by cable car to the Rifugio Montagnola, from where you can continue on foot or in a Jeep. Tour agencies offer full day excursions to Mount Etna from Taormina; the tourist office there can provide information *(see page 127)*.

The volcano on Strómboli puts on an around-the-clock performance: Every 20 minutes or so, the crater hurls glowing multi-coloured chunks of lava into the sky and down a cliff called the Sciara del Fuoco into the sea, where they hiss and steam. You can witness this spectacle from a viewpoint that is a safe distance from the activity and reached by an easy-to-climb, well-marked path; a guided ascent takes you closer to the action and is most rewarding at night. You can also view the spectacle from boats that leave from the island's tiny port, where several private agencies offer tours and provide information on how to view the volcano by land or sea.

MUSIC AND THE PERFORMING ARTS

Some of the most memorable performances in Sicily are the seasonal events held in the island's Greek theaters and other historic locations. Check with local tourist boards *(see page 127)* for lists of events.

Throughout the summer in **Catania**, Baroque churches and an outdoor stage in Piazza Bellini are the settings for concerts of classical and popular music, and the Teatro Metropolitana and Teatro Nuovo host a jazz festival that runs from November through April. The city's Teatro Bellini, named after the famous operatic composer Vincenzo Bellini, is a world-famous

venue for operas from October through May.

Caos (outside Agrigento) pays tribute to Luigi Pirandello, a native son, with performances of his plays in July.

Erice's churches and other venues open their doors for performances of medieval

You'll have plenty of opportunities to pursue a little Sicilian fun in the sun.

and Renaissance music throughout the summer. Erice becomes known for music again the first Sunday in December, when the town welcomes a festival of traditional folk music.

The mosaic-filled cathedral in **Monreale** is the setting for a festival of ecclesiastic music during the first week of November.

Noto's Baroque churches and convents are the venues for the International Music Festival in July and August; the Teatro Communale hosts concerts from January through June.

In **Palermo**, the Teatro Massimo in Piazza Verdi is once again welcoming concertgoers, and other concerts are performed in churches around the city.

Classical dramas are staged in **Segesta**'s Greek theatre throughout the summer.

In even-numbered years, **Siracusa** stages a festival of classical drama in its Greek theatre.

The Greek theatre in **Taormina** draws visitors from around the world for a festival of classical music and dance from July through mid-September.

Classic Greek drama graces the stage of the Greek theatre in **Tindari** in July and August.

In **Trapani**, the tropical gardens of the Villa Margherita are the setting for a music festival in July.

Puppet Theatre

This lively entertainment, with its elaborate costumes, non-stop action and touches of humour, has been delighting Sicilian children and adults for centuries. Even audiences who don't speak Italian and aren't familiar with the tales, which are usually based on exploits of knights in the court of Charlemagne, find this spectacle engrossing. In Palermo, the Museo Internazionale delle Marionette regularly stages performances, and puppets from around the world are on display. The Museo Etnográfico Siciliano Pitrè, in Palermo's

Parco della Favorita, also has a collection of puppets and a puppet theatre that sometimes hosts performances.

A puppet show is usually part of the festivities at fairs and other public celebrations in Sicily. Travelling troops tour the island in the summer, often making stops in the resorts. Local tourist offices can let you know where and when you can find performances.

TRAVELLING WITH CHILDREN

Sicilians shower attention on their children, and will probably do the same with yours. Welcome as children are in museums, restaurants and just about any other place in Sicily, you may want to seek out some activities that will provide a break from trudging through ruins and archaeological museums. Some suggestions:

In **Palermo** a walk through the Vucciria market will provide plenty of diversions, as will a look at the Cala, the old fishing harbour. The Arab and Norman sights, with their whiff of exoticism, will be popular — especially the cathedral in Monreale, with its mosaics and cloisters, and the church of San Giovanni degli Eremiti, with it gardens.

Cefalù and **Taormina** are pleasant to visit with children, because the low-key, car-free old towns provide plenty of diversions (especially the Greek theatre and views of Mount Etna in Taormina), and both beaches and countryside are nearby. **Erice** is also a good place for young travellers to unwind, and they can wander the medieval streets, explore the ruined castle and enjoy the stunning views.

Of the classical sights, **Selinunte** is the most child-friendly, because of the lack of crowds and its nearby beaches and adjoining fishing port. With their volcanic peaks, black sand beaches and blue waters, the **Aeolian Islands** might appear like a magic kingdom to youngsters (after all, this archipel-

The Trapani seafront is most enjoyable because it provides a jumping-off point for trips to the Egadi Islands.

ago has inspired many a myth) and the trip from island to island on ferry can be fun. **Strómboli**, with its ever-active volcano, is sure to please. Of course, an ascent up **Mount Etna** is mandatory; a trip around its lower flanks on the Circumetna railway may be the best approach if the young ones aren't up to arduous treks across the lava. The Roman mosaics at **Casale** will enchant even a sight-weary child, especially the ones depicting children at play.

Parents with very young children in tow may want to avoid the treasures of churches, which are often filled with withered extremities and other ghoulish relics. A visit to **Palermo**'s Catacombe del Convento dei Cappuccini, where thousands of preserved corpses are draped about the premises, may or may not be appropriate, depending on a child's age and sensitivities. The catacombs in **Siracusa**, meanwhile, are corpse-less but spooky nonetheless.

EATING OUT

Sicilian cuisine will probably be among the more pleasurable discoveries you make on the island. In general, it is lighter, spicier and healthier than the cuisines of many other parts of Italy. Cooks rely heavily on the three staples that are plentiful on the island: vegetables that grow year-round, fish, especially *tonno* (tuna) and *pesce spada* (swordfish), and olive oil. Capers, raisins, wild fennel and ingredients that are often the legacy of the island's Arab heritage lend a faintly exotic flavour to many dishes, and even couscous creeps onto menus in the south and west of the island.

Meat is a presence on menus, but not nearly as important a part of the local cuisine as it is to cooking elsewhere in Italy. Instead, pasta sauces are often made with vegetables and fish, especially fresh sardines and anchovies. Perhaps the island's best-known culinary contribution is *Spaghetti alla Norma*, named for the heroine of the opera by native son Vincenzo Bellini and made with eggplant, tomatoes and fresh ricotta. Sicilian desserts are delicious, and are often made with almonds and the fresh fruit that grows in such abundance on the island.

Where to Eat

Restaurants are usually referred to as *trattoria* or *ristorante,* and though the terms have come to denote establishments of similar character, in principal at least they are quite different. A trattoria is casual, serving homey fare in an informal setting; a ristorante implies smarter décor, more polished service and more elaborate and more expensive cuisine. Some of the more formal establishments in Palermo and Taormina effect the ambiance of the latter, but most Sicilian eateries are of the family-run trattoria variety.

On the Lìpari, an outdoor café is perfect for people-watching.

Bars in Sicily and elsewhere in Italy are not just places to drink alcoholic beverages. They sell wine and spirits, as well as soft drinks, mineral water and coffee. They also serve light fare: pastries *(cornetti or brioche)* both of which are croissants filled with jam, custard, or chocolate in the morning, little sandwiches *(tramezzino)* and filled flat rolls *(panini)* or other light dishes throughout the day. All these foods are usually displayed on the counter, you need only point to what you want.

Many Sicilians will stop by their local bar several times a day for a quick coffee and chat, and you should find one you like and do the same — there's almost no better place in which to observe the engaging drama of day-to-day Sicilian life. You will be more welcome in a bar if you observe a rule that seems to confuse most non-Italians: never try to pay the serving people behind the counter. Instead, decide what you want to eat and drink and pay the cashier in advance; the cashier will give you a receipt that you present to the servers behind the bar when you tell them what you would like.

Yet another type of eating establishment is the *tavola calda* or *rosticceria,* both of which are cafeteria-style eateries where several selections of hot dishes are prepared daily and served from a counter. You generally pay in advance and take the receipt to someone behind the counter, who prepares a plate for you. *Pizzerias* appear in every Sicilian town, and often prepare their pizzas in wood-burning ovens; toppings in Sicily often include sardines, anchovies, fresh vegetables and mozzarella.

A *caffè* and its kindred *pasticcerie* usually serve pastries and other sweets (often ice cream, or *gelato*) and sometimes light meals, accompanied by coffee, tea, or a glass of wine. An establishment or two like this grace the main piazzas of most towns in Sicily. In Palermo, two popular cafés are the Opera on Piazza Verdi opposite the Teatro Massimo and the nearby Mazzara, on Via Generale Magliocco 15.

Coffee Break

A smell you will notice all over Sicily is that of coffee. When it comes to ordering this ubiquitous beverage, you have several options. A *caffè* is a single shot of espresso, dispensed from an elaborate-looking espresso-maker behind the bar. A double shot is *una doppia.* Coffee topped with steamed, frothy milk is *cappuccino;* incidentally, Italians consider cappuccino to be a morning-only drink and find the notion of ordering one after lunch or dinner ridiculous. *Caffè machiato* is espresso with just a drop of steamed milk; *caffè latte* is espresso mixed with a generous serving of warm milk; *caffè corretto* is espresso with a shot of alcohol. While coffee is by far the more popular choice, tea *(tè)* is widely available, served with milk *(con latte)* or lemon *(con limone)* and iced *(tè freddo)* in summer.

One more essential stop when travelling in Sicily is a *gelateria,* a shop that sells only *gelato* (ice cream) and *sorbetto,* which is usually made with fresh fruit. Some distinctive Sicilian flavours are jasmine *(gelsomino)* and mulberry *(gelsi).* When choosing a gelateria, look for lines of locals (who usually know where to find the best gelato in town) and for a sign that says *produzione propria,* which means 'made on the premises'. No trip to Mondello, the seaside retreat near Palermo, is complete without a stop at Renato, a famous gelateria in the centre of town on Piazza Mondello.

A ristorante or trattoria usually serves both lunch and dinner; rare is the one that doesn't serve both. In Sicily, lunch is from 1pm to 3 or 3:30pm, and dinner from 8 to 10:30pm. A restaurant will occasionally keep later hours, but rarely past 11pm or so. Most establishments close one day a week and occasionally for lunch or dinner immediately preceding or following the closing — so a restaurant that is closed on Monday may also close for Sunday dinner or Tuesday lunch. In the resorts, however, many restaurants keep longer hours in summer, and some close from November to March. Cafés are usually open from 8am to 11pm; bars tend to keep longer hours, especially in busy resort towns, from 7am or so until as late as 2am.

Fruit is abundant in Sicily, especially at markets like this one in Catania.

The schedule an establishment follows is usually well-posted near the front door, with a sign showing hours, weekly closing days and annual closing dates. Most also post their menus and prices out front. In so doing, they provide you with the opportunity to see what you will be getting into before you wander into a restaurant and sit down.

Most restaurants in Sicily include a service charge in the bill (usually 10 percent of the total), and many add a small *coperto* (cover charge) as well. If the service is satisfactory, leave a little extra, perhaps a euro or two (and service in Sicily tends to be excellent).

What to Eat

You will notice that just about all menus are divided into more or less the same categories (to an Italian, these are the essential elements of a decent meal): *antipasti* (appetisers), *primi* (first courses), *secondi* (second courses), *contorni* (side dishes) and *dolci* (desserts).

While many Italian diners will include all of these elements in a meal, ordering a pasta dish or a secondo and a contorno is acceptable, especially at lunch. A meal in Sicily is to be enjoyed and lingered over, and the experience is all the better if you dine outdoors, an experience that is commonplace because of the island's balmy climate.

Fresh ingredients provide the key to Sicilian cuisine.

Following are some of the items you are likely to find on many Sicilian menus.

Antipasto means 'before the meal', and these selections are usually served cold and in small portions. Many restaurants offer an *antipasto mista* (mixed antipasto) that is served buffet-style from a table laden with such dishes as *prosciutto con melone* (ham and melon) or *prosciutto crudo con fichi* (ham with figs) and *insalata caprese* (mozzarella, tomatoes and basil).

Typical Sicilian antipasti: *Arancine,* fried rice balls stuffed with meat or cheese; *Caponata,* a salad made with eggplant (aubergines), olives, capers and celery; *Crocché,* fried cheese and potato dumplings; *Panella,* a fritter of ceci (chickpeas); *Sfincione,* a pizza-like concoction in which thick bread is topped with tomatoes, onions and anchovies.

Primo is the first course, and in Sicily that generally means pasta, which is often made with fresh seafood, and occasionally soup.

Cool-down terms: When ordering a beverage, you might want to ask for *ghiaccio* (ice) and *spicchio di limone* (slice of lemon).

Typical Sicilian primi: *Maccu,* a creamy soup made from chickpeas. Or pasta like: *Pasta all'arrabbiata,* a spicy sauce of tomatoes and anchovies; *Pasta con broccoli,* with fresh broccoli and often anchovies; *Pasta con la mollica,* pasta with breadcrumbs, capers, olives and anchovies; *Pasta con seppia,* with cuttlefish served in its own ink; *Pasta con le sarde,* with fresh sardines, raisins, fennel and pine nuts; *Spaghetti alla Norma,* with tomato, basil, fried eggplant *(aubergine)* and ricotta cheese; *Spaghetti al peperoncino,* with chilli pepper and garlic; and *Spaghetti alla Trapanese,* tossed with tomatoes, garlic and basil.

Secondo is the main dish, which in Sicily is often fish, though chicken, veal, lamb and pork also appear on menus. *Pesce spada* (swordfish), caught in Sicilian waters, makes an appearance on menus all over the island, and is often grilled. *Tonno* (tuna) is also common, and is caught off the island as well.

Typical Sicilian secondi: *Calamari ripieni alla griglia,* grilled squid filled with a stuffing of raisins, capers, garlic, pine nuts and anchovies; *Cuscus,* a North African import common in western Sicily, served with a vegetable sauce; *Cuscus con pesce,* the same dish topped with *zuppa di pesce; Fritto misto,* a platter of fried clams, squid, cuttlefish, sardines and other seafood, depending (in a good restaurant) on what's fresh; *Involtini di pesce spada,* rolled swordfish cooked in breadcrumbs and oil; *Scaloppine di vitello al Marsala,* veal scaloppini cooked in Marsala wine (chicken, or *pollo,* and pork, or *maiale,* are also often prepared this way); *Zuppa di pesce,* usually made with clams, mussels, squid and sometimes chunks of tuna or swordfish in a thick sauce of tomatoes, wine and olive oil.

> When in a bar, it is customary to pay the cashier first, then place your order with the server behind the counter

Contorno is the vegetable course. It's almost always ordered separately, as vegetables and salad are usually not included with a secondo. Sicily produces a wide variety of vegetables year-round; usually only a few items are offered, but they are almost always fresh from the market that day. Some common vegetables include *carciofi,* artichokes; *ceci,* chick peas; *fagioli,* beans, usually especially white beans; *finocchio,* fennel; *melanzane,* eggplant (aubergines); *peperoni,* peppers; and *zucchini* (courgettes). Salads, *insalata,* are straightforward and tend to come in two varieties: *insalata verde,* a simple green salad, or *insalata mista,* greens with mixed vegetables. A delicious salad that appears on some menus is with *arance e finocchio,* oranges and fennel.

Dolci are desserts. Sicilians excel at making sweets, and restaurants on the island often offer desserts that are only found in Sicily. Typical Sicilian dolci: *Cannoli,* fried pastry tubes filled with ricotta and candied fruit; *Cassata,* a light cake filled with ricotta, candied fruit, chopped pistachio and chocolate; *Crespelle di riso,* pancakes made with sweetened rice; and *Frutta di Martorana,* also called *pasta reale,* fruit shaped marzipan.

In markets, apricots and cherries beg to be eaten.

Beverages

Most Sicilians prefer to drink mineral water *(acqua minerale).* You will be asked in restaurants if you want one of three types of water: *acqua normale,* which is from the tap; *acqua frissante, con gas,* or *gassata,* all of which mean mineral water 'with gas', which English speakers might know better as 'sparkling water'; and *acqua naturale* or *non gassata,* which is mineral water without gas.

While canned soft drinks *(analcóliche)* are common — Coke and Fanta lemon or orange drinks (Fanta *limone* or *arance)* are probably the most prevalent — don't overlook some of the more interesting alternatives that are available in Sicily. *Spermuta* is a fresh-squeezed juice, made with oranges *(arance)* and lemons *(limone)* grown on the island and a sure-fire remedy for the effects of summer heat; if you order a *spermuta di limone,* you will want to add sugar and water to your taste. A Sicilian speciality is *granita,* a sorbet made with crushed ice that is flavoured with the fresh juice of lemons, strawberries or other fruits or, sometimes sweetened coffee.

Italian beer is excellent; ask for a *birra nazionale* and you will probably be served a bottle of Peroni or a Messina, which is brewed in Sicily. Many imported brands are also available, especially Kronenberg and Heineken. Draft beer *(birra alla spina)* is often imported and more expensive than you might expect.

Spirits are widely available, and are served neat, without ice, unless you ask for it *(ghiaccio)*. The island also makes several rather sticky and bitter, herbal tasting liqueurs, including Averna, which is made in Caltanissetta, and Fichera, from the slopes of Mount Etna. Some of the island's lemon harvest finds its way into *limoncello,* another syrupy after-dinner drink.

Wine

Sicily's most famous wine — and long one of its most famous exports — is Marsala, a fortified wine comparable to Port or Sherry. It's been produced since the 18th century near the city on the southwestern coast from which it takes

Rating the Wines

In Sicily as elsewhere in Italy, wines are classified with three ratings. DOCG *(Denominazione di Origine Controllata Garantita)* indicates that a wine is from an established wine-producing region and maintains consistently high standards of quality. DOC *(Denominazione di Origine Controllata)* ensures that a wine is from an established area and meets the standards of that area — a DOC wine is guaranteed to be a quality wine, but will be of a lesser quality than a DOCG wine. The third classification is *vino di tavola,* which more or less denotes that a wine is a good table wine from a reputable producer.

its name and is drunk as an aperitif or with or after dessert. Bars and restaurants in Marsala serve their own variation of their local drink, *Marsala all'uovo,* to which they add a little sugar and a raw egg.

Sweet elixirs, in fact, are something of a Sicilian speciality. Malvasia is another dessert wine made in the Aeolian Islands and the island of Pantelleria produces Moscato di Pantelleria Naturale, made from Zibibbo grapes that are fermented in the sun. Taormina produces vino alla Mandorla, a wine made from almonds.

Of course, Sicily also produces some excellent table wines. Many travellers may already be familiar with the island's red and white Corvos, which are exported around the world and are available throughout the island as well. Etna is produced from grapes grown on volcanic soil in the foothills of the volcano and is available as

> One drink you can't get at some bars in Sicily is a glass of wine; in many places wine can only be served by the bottle.

red, white or rosé. Some wines that are little known outside Sicily but are well worth looking for are Alcamo, from around Trapani, and Cerasuolo di Vittoria, from vineyards outside Ragusa. Restaurants in the island's major cities often serve wines that come from nearby vineyards, and they are well worth trying: Donnafugata in Palermo, Terreforti in Siracusa and Anapo in Siracusa.

Useful Restaurant Terms

Here are a few terms that may enhance your dining experiences. Be bold: Your efforts at speaking Italian will be much appreciated.

Buona sera.	Good afternoon/evening.
Parla inglese?	Do you speak English?

Aperto	Open
Chiuso	Closed
Prima colazione	Breakfast
Pranzo	Lunch
Cena	Dinner
Avete un menu?	Do you have a menu?
Quanto costa?	How much is it?
Il conto, per favore.	The bill, please.

Avete una tavola per una/due/tre/quattro persona/persone?
Do you have a table for one/two/three/four people?

In addition to the regional specialities discussed on pages 96–99, here are some common terms you are likely to encounter on Sicilian menus:

aglio	garlic	*formaggio*	cheese
agnello	lamb	*frittata*	omelet
baccalaru	Sicilian for	*frutti di mare*	seafood
	baccalà,	*funghi*	mushrooms
	salted cod	*gamberetti*	shrimp
basilico	basil	*insalata*	salad
birra	beer	*lepre*	hare
burro	butter	*lumache*	snails
cacocciulo	Sicilian for	*maiale*	pork
	carciofo,	*melanzane*	aubergine
	artichoke	*panna*	cream
caffè	coffee	*pane*	bread
calamari	squid	*patate*	potatoes
ceci	chickpeas	*peperoni*	peppers
cipolle	onions	*pesce*	fish
coniglio	rabbit	*piccione*	pigeon
cozze	mussels	*pollo*	chicken
fagioli	beans	*polipo*	octopus
fegato	liver	*pomodori*	tomatoes

finnochio	fennel	*primo sale*	a sweet cheese
prosciutto	ham	*spiedino*	skewers of meat
rognoni	kidneys	*spinachi*	spinach
siccia	Sicilian for *seppia,* cuttlefish	*tè*	tea
		vitello	veal
		uova	eggs

Some Typical Pastas

fettucine	long, flat, narrow strips	*penne*	short tubes
orecchiette	ear-shaped pasta	*tagliatelle*	flat egg noodles
pappardelle	wide, short noodles	*vermicelli*	thin spaghetti

Some Common Pasta Sauces

alla Norma	with eggplant
alla panna	with cream
arrabbiata	hot tomato sauce, often with salted anchovies
bolognese	meat sauce
napolitana	with tomato and basil
pesto	a mixture of basil, garlic, and pine nuts
vongole	with clams, garlic and oil

Plenty of restaurants offer sumpuous seafood dinners with sea views.

HANDY TRAVEL TIPS

An A–Z Summary of Practical Information

A

ACCOMMODATION

Most lodgings in Sicily are called *albergo* or *hotel,* which connote exactly the same kind of hostelry. *Pensione* is also used frequently, and this term traditionally suggests a small, family-run establishment. A *locanda* is usually a rural inn, but this term can also connote a simple establishment in an urban setting.

However an accommodation is labelled, it falls into one of the five levels (indicated by stars) of the government rating system. The number of stars reflects the number of amenities offered (in-room bathrooms, elevators, air-conditioning, etc.); the more stars a hotel has been assigned, the more amenities it offers. The star system is strictly objective and does not reflect charm or ambiance. Accordingly, a five-star hotel can be a well-equipped modern hotel in Palermo catering to business people or a lavish resort in Taormina. In general, the more stars a hotel is given, the more expensive it will be. Tourist offices *(see page 127)* can provide a detailed list of accommodation, with addresses, phone and fax numbers, number of rooms, amenities and prices.

In general, the choice of hotels is fairly limited outside of Palermo and the resorts of Cefalù and Taormina. This doesn't mean you can't find good lodgings elsewhere on the island but in many cities and towns the options are fairly basic.

Farm accommodation called *agriturismi* are becoming increasingly common in Sicily. To be labelled as such, an *agriturismo* must have fewer than 30 beds, and the property must earn most of its income from agricultural pursuits. Accommodation and prices can vary greatly (and are not rated by the hotel system). In most you will be served a country breakfast with local cheeses and other products, and you may be served other meals (almost always featuring homegrown ingredients). Tourist boards can provide information on *agriturismi*, and for farm accommodation throughout Sicily or websites www.sicilia-agriturismo.com and www.agriturist.it.

Sicily

Many residents of the Aeolian and Egadi Islands rent rooms in their homes. Appearing on the dock with bags in hand may well initiate an onslaught of eager hosts, or you can ask at a bar or local travel agency. Look for signs announcing *camere libre* (room for rent).

You can book a long-term rental in advance, although apartments and houses are likely to be available only in such major resorts as Taormina and Cefalù, as well as in the nearby islands. Tourist boards sometimes provide information on such rentals, and they can also direct you to local real estate companies that handle short-term rental properties. Before you turn over a deposit, ask to see a contract with terms thoroughly spelled out, photos and the names of previous renters with whom you can speak.

I'd like a single/double bed.	**Vorrei una camera singola/matrimoniale** or **doppia.**
With bath/shower	**Con bagno/doccia**
What is the price per night?	**Qual è il prezzo per una notte?**

AIRPORTS *(Aeroporti)*

Sicily is served by two main airports, one in Palermo and one in Catania. A smaller airport in Trapani handles flights within Sicily. Although Palermo is larger than Catania and the capital of the island, Catania's airport is larger and served by more flights.

The airports in Palermo and Catania do not accommodate nonstop flights from North America or other distant countries. They are, however, well connected to major airports elsewhere in Italy with frequent service to and from Rome, Milan and Naples. Both also serve flights from airports in London and other European cities, though many of these connect through Rome, Milan, or Naples as well. Travellers from North America, Australia, New Zealand, or other overseas countries can often fly nonstop to one of the major Italian airports or an airline's major hub elsewhere in Europe and continue on to Palermo or Catania from there.

Palermo's Aeroporto Falcone Borsellino is 30km (18 miles) west of the city in Punta Raisi; Tel. (091) 685-723. Buses leave from in front of the terminal for the 45-minute trip to the city center, departing roughly every half hour from 5am to the time of the last arrival of the day; you can purchase a ticket on the bus (the one-way fare is about 5 euros). Many hire car agencies, including international firms, have outlets at the airport.

Catania's Aeroporto Fontanarosso is 5km (3 miles) outside the city center; Tel. (095) 730-6277. Buses leave from outside the terminal for the 20-minute trip to Piazza Stesicoro in the centre of the city and to Stazione Centrale, departing roughly every 20 minutes from 5:30am to midnight; you can purchase a ticket from a newsstand inside the terminal (the one-way fare is 5 euros). Buses from the airport also make connections to Siracusa, Ragusa, Taormina and many other cities in eastern Sicily, as well as Palermo. From Catania's train station it is also easy to reach Siracusa, Taormina and other cities in Sicily. There are many hire car outlets at the airport.

When is the next plane to…?	**A che ora parte il prossimo aereo per…?**
I would like a ticket for…	**Vorrei un biglietto per…**
Please take these bags to the train/bus/taxi.	**Mi porti queste vallge fino al treno/all'aotobus/al taxi, per favore.**

BUDGETING FOR YOUR TRIP

When determining your budget, think of Palermo and Taormina and the rest of Sicily as two separate entities. Hotels in Palermo can be as expensive as those in Rome, and lodgings in Taormina are on par with those in Positano; accommodation elsewhere in Sicily is moderate in terms of cost. In Palermo you can expect to pay 180 to 250 euros for standard double accommodation. Outside of Palermo or Taormina, you can probably find a similar room for 100 to 200 euros.

Sicily

Meals are not terribly expensive in Sicily; you can usually enjoy an excellent meal for two (excluding wine) for about 25 euros; a lunch of pizza or a salad for two will be about half that. Entry fees to museums and archaeological sites average 5 euros.

CAMPING

Camping is permitted only in designated areas, of which there are about 90 in Sicily. Most are on the coast and on the Aeolian and Egadi Islands. Tourist boards include campgrounds in their accommodation listings, and the Italian State Tourist Office produces a booklet on camping in Sicily, *Sicilia Campeggi*.

CAR HIRE *(Autonoleggio)*

One sure way to save money when hiring a car in Sicily is to make arrangements before leaving home; in doing so, you will be ensured rates that are usually half of what they would be if you hired a car on the spot. Most major companies have outlets at the airports in Palermo and Catania and in the centres of both cities, as well as in some of the major resorts. They provide competitive rates, especially for rentals of a week or more. Expect to pay considerably more (often double) for a car with automatic transmission and air-conditioning. A tax of 19% is added to all car rentals, as is a surcharge of 10% if you pick up your car and drop it off at the airport.

CLIMATE

Sicily enjoys good weather year round, with mild winters and hot summers. The only extremes you can expect are in July and August, when daytime temperatures of 40º C (95º F) are not unusual. The southern coast is the warmest place on the island, and it is often buffeted by hot sirocco winds that blow in off the Sahara. November and December can be rainy. Spring arrives early, in March, and the island is unusually pleasant at this time because wildflowers bloom everywhere. Below are average temperatures in Palermo, accurate for most of the island except in the cooler mountainous interior and on the southern coast in the summer.

	J	F	M	A	M	J	J	A	S	O	N	D
°C	10.5	10.5	13	16	18.5	23	25.5	25	23	20	17	12.5
°F	52	52	55	61	73	78	77	73	68	62	62	56

CLOTHING

Sicilians have become inured to the sight of tourists clad in shorts and t-shirts tromping through their piazzas. The locals dress well and some-what conservatively, and they will treat you with a little more respect if you dress as they do — trousers and short-sleeved shirts for men in the summer, and trousers and blouses, skirts, or dresses for women. Walking shorts are appropriate, but never wear bathing attire off the beach and don't wear skimpy attire of any sort when visiting churches.

Since summertime temperatures can soar to near 40° C (low 100's F), pack clothing made of light fabric. From November through March you will need a sweater or light jacket in the cool evenings and a raincoat for the frequent showers. Only a few of the more expensive restaurants require jacket-and-tie formality, but you will want to dress well, even if casually so, for dinner. For women shorts and sleeveless t-shirts are not proper attire for a church visit — in fact, at the largest, most-visited churches a guard is posted at the front door to check for immodest attire.

CRIME AND SAFETY

Petty crime against tourists is fairly common in Sicily, especially pick-pocketing and purse- and jewellery-snatching. Car theft is also fairly common, as is the theft of goods from within a parked car. Some precautions to take:

Leave passports, jewellery, large amounts of cash, credit cards you are not using and other valuables in the hotel safe (many hotels provide them in the rooms; if not, ask to check valuables at the desk).

Keep a copy of your passport and other valuable documents sepa-rately in case you need to replace them. Also, keep an extra credit card or ATM card apart from the others (for instance, carry one with you, keep others in the safe); this way you will have a fallback.

Wear a money belt or keep your money and credit cards in a front pocket or some other place where a pickpocket cannot get at them easily, especially at markets, street festivals and other occasions where large crowds congregate.

Never leave valuables in view within your car; whenever possible, park in an attended lot (most archaeological sites and other attractions have them).

To protect yourself against Vespa-riding bandits, who snatch bags while whizzing by at high speed, carry a bag so it faces away from the street.

I want to report a theft.	**Voglio denunciare un furto.**
My wallet/passport/ticket has been stolen.	**Mi hanno rubato il portafoglio/ il passaporto/il biglietto.**

CUSTOMS *(Dogana)* AND ENTRY REQUIREMENTS

Citizens of EU countries need only a valid passport or an identity card to enter Italy. Citizens of the US, Canada, Australia, New Zealand and South Africa need only a valid passport, though a special visa or resident permit is required for stays of more than 90 days. To facilitate the replacement process in case you lose your passport while travelling, photocopy the first page of your passport twice; leave one copy at home and keep another with you, but separately from the passport.

EU regulations now allow for the free exchange of goods for personal use between member countries. For residents of non-EU countries, the following restrictions apply:

Currency restrictions and the IVA Tax. While there is no limit on the amount of currency you can bring into Italy, you must declare any currency over the amount of about 2,500 euros upon leaving the country.

IVA. A Value Added Tax of 12–19% is added to all purchases in Italy. In many cases, residents of non-EU countries can claim a refund for part of this tax on purchases of more than about 75 euros at one store — if they are willing to follow some complex procedures. These involve having customs officials at the airport stamp the receipt as you depart Italy and mailing the stamped receipt back to the store within 90 days of purchase; the store will mail you a refund. A simpler 'Tax Free for Tourists' plan is now being adopted by many stores: The store will issue you a receipt and check, which you can redeem at the airport once you present your receipt to customs and have it stamped.

Into:	cigarettes	cigars		tobacco	alcohol		wine		beer
Australia:	250	250	*or*	250g	1*l*				
Canada:	200 *and*	50	*and*	400g	1.14*l*	*or*	1.1*l*	*or*	8.5*l*
New Zealand:	200 *or*	50	*or*	250g	1*l*	*and*	4.5*l*	*or*	4.5*l*
South Africa:	400 *and*	50	*and*	250g	1*l*	*and*	2*l*		
USA:	200 *or*	50	*or*	2kg	1*l*	*or*	1*l*		

D

DRIVING

Sicily has a good network of well-maintained and well-marked roads. A system of four-lane toll roads *(autostradi)* traverses parts of the island. A20 runs along the north shore from Messina to Cefalù where it joins the A19 to Palermo. The A18 runs along the east coast between Messina and Catania; the A19 cuts through the middle of the island from Catania to Enna and Palermo; and the A29 traverses the northwestern quadrant of the island and connects Palermo and Trapani. The maximum speed (rarely observed) on the autostrada is 130km/h (80mph). Slower traffic should keep to the right and venture into the left lane only when passing (overtaking); should you linger there, inevitably a faster-moving car will roar up from behind flashing its headlights, an indication to move over quickly.

Sicily

Smaller roads on Sicily are also well maintained, and you will want to use them to see the island's beautiful countryside. Driving in cities is stress-producing, to say the least, and you are well-advised not to drive in the traffic-crowded centers of Palermo and Catania. The speed limit on secondary roads is 90km/h (55mph); in towns, it's 50km/h (30mph). Wherever you drive in Sicily, the major hazards are your fellow motorists, who tend to drive fast and often recklessly. Two words of advice: Drive defensively.

Drive on the right (for this reason, motorists from the UK may want to hire a car in Italy rather than using their own) and pass on the left. At intersections and traffic circles (roundabouts), traffic on the right has the right of way.

Drivers from the US, Canada, the UK, Australia, New Zealand and South Africa require only a valid driver's licence from their home countries (an international driver's permit is no longer required). Motorists bringing their own cars into Italy must have an official nationality sticker displayed in the rear of the vehicle, an international motor insurance certificate and a vehicle registration document. EU residents must have a green insurance card, which will greatly facilitate matters in case of an accident. Drivers and all passengers must wear seat belts, and motorcyclists must wear helmets. All cars must be equipped with a red warning triangle in case of breakdown. If you bring a car into Italy from the UK or the Republic of Ireland you must adjust the headlights (lamps) for right-side driving.

In case of an accident or breakdown, dial 113 (your call will probably be answered by someone who does not speak English, so have a translator at your side) or the Automobile Club of Italy at 116 (where your call may be answered by an English speaker). Roadside phones, usually yellow, are placed at frequent intervals along major roads.

It is usually difficult (and often illegal) to park on the street in towns and cities. Look at signs carefully — parking is often restricted to residents only, or you will be required to pay for parking at a curbside machine, which will deliver a receipt (indicating the time of expiration) that you must display in full view on the dashboard. Many Sicilian cities and towns have municipal parking lots and garages, denoted by a white 'P' on a blue background, at the fringes of their historic centers; use these whenever possible.

Petrol is readily available (though off the autostradi many stations close for lunch from noon to 3pm) and expensive by non-European standards. Diesel is readily available too. It is available in three grades: *super, normale and senza pombo* (unleaded).

Signage on all roads is excellent. Some common terms you are likely to encounter (and these will usually be accompanied by the international symbol) are:

Curva pericolosa	Dangerous curve
Deviazione	Detour (diversion)
Divieto di sorpasso	No passing (overtaking)
Divieto di sosta	No stopping
Lavori in corso	Men working (road works)
Pericolo	Danger
Rallentare	Slow down
Senso vietato/unico	No entry/one-way street
Vleto l'ingresso	No entry
Zona pedonale	Pedestrian zone
Zona traffico limita	Limited traffic zone

Some useful phrases:

Driver's licence	**Patente**
Car registration papers	**Libretto di circolazione**
Green insurance card	**Carte verde**
Can I park here?	**Posso parcheggiare qui?**
Are we on the right road for…?	**Siamo sulla strada giusta per…?**

Fill the tank, please, with…	**Per favore, faccia il pieno de…**
I've had a breakdown.	**Ho avuto un guasto.**
There's been an accident.	**C'è stato un incidente.**

E

ELECTRICITY

220V/50Hz is standard. Visitors from other countries may require an adaptor *(una presa complementare),* and those from North America will need a converter as well. Better hotels often have special outlets for some North American appliances.

EMBASSIES AND CONSULATES

These offices are the places to go if you lose your passport, are embroiled in police or other bureaucratic dealings, or are otherwise in need of assistance. The US Consulate in Palermo is at Via Re Frederico 18b, Tel. (091) 611 0020; the UK Consulate is at Via Cavour 121, Tel. (091) 582 533. Citizens of other English-speaking countries can turn to their embassies in Rome: Australia, Via Alessandria 215, Tel. (06) 852 721; Canada, Via G. B. de Rossi 27, Tel. (06) 445 981; New Zealand, Via Zara 28, Tel. (06) 441 7171; Republic of Ireland, Largo del Nazareno 3, Tel. (06) 697 9121; and South Africa, Via Tanaro 14, Tel. (06) 841 9794.

EMERGENCIES

The general emergency number is 113. Call 112 for the *carabinieri* (national police), 115 for the fire department and 118 for an ambulance.

Please, can you place an emergency call for me to the…?

Per favore, può fare me una telefonata d'emergenza…?

police	**alla polizia**	ambulance	**ambulanza**
Fire!	**Al fuoco!**	hospital	**al'ospedale**
fire brigade	**ai pompieri**		

G

GAY AND LESBIAN TRAVELLERS

Sicily is one of Italy's more conservative regions, and in general Sicilians are not as tolerant of homosexuality as are residents of northern Italy and many other parts of Europe. Taormina is one of the few places in Sicily with anything approaching a gay scene, and even that is quite circumspect. It's not that Sicilians won't welcome same-sex partners travelling together; they will, however, frown on public displays of affection that exceeds the warmth that often exists between members of the same sex here and elsewhere in southern Italy.

GETTING THERE

By Air

Travellers coming to Sicily from outside of Italy can fly into Rome or Milan and connect there for flights to Palermo or Catania. Travellers from Great Britain can also fly into Pisa and make connections there. No matter where you are coming from outside of Italy, you will usually have to make at least one connection to reach Sicily.

Alitalia, Italy's national airline, has service to Rome and Milan (with connections to Catania and Palermo), from New York, Miami, Chicago and Los Angeles, offering daily flights to and from most of these cities. British Airways offers daily flights to Catania and Palermo from London and other British cities, often with connections in Rome, Milan, or Pisa; Alitalia also flies from London to Catania and Palermo, with similar connections. Alitalia runs several nonstops a week to Rome (with connections to Catania and Palermo) from Sydney and Johannesburg.

Another option for travellers coming from overseas is to fly to a European airline's hub and connect to flights for Sicily from there. Air France, Air Malta, British Airways, KLM/Northwest, Lufthansa, Sabena and SAS are among the airlines that provide service to Sicily via connections through their European hubs and a stopover or connection in Rome or Milan.

Sicily

When planning a trip, remember that, in airline terminology, high season (when rates are highest) is from June into early September; shoulder season, when prices are substantially lower than they are in high season, is from April through May and early or mid-September through October, and low season is November through March — with the notable exceptions of Christmas and Easter, when fares return to high-season levels. To give you an idea of how much fares can fluctuate within these seasons, a round-trip ticket from New York to Palermo can be $1,000 or more in high season and less than $300 in low season.

Budget Options. In general, the most economical fares are APEX, which usually require an advance purchase of 14 to 21 days and are valid for stays of 7–30 days; fares are almost always lower for midweek departures. The lowest fares are usually available in the slowest travel times extremely low fares are often available in early November, early December and January through March. The least expensive fares are those offered low-cost airlines that fly from the UK to Palermo and Catania; they offer the most flights in the summer.

By Train
Daily express trains link Rome with Palermo, Catania and Siracusa; at the Strait of Messina, the train cars are detached and put onto a ferry for the crossing to Messina in Sicily. The trip, however, is long — about ten hours from Rome to Palermo, and it's about 40 hours by train from London to Palermo. For schedules and general information, contact the Italian State Tourist Board *(see page 127)* or CIT, which is the travel arm of Ferrovia della Stato (the Italian state railway); Tel. 800-223-7987 (toll-free) in the US, 081-686-0677 in the UK and 02-267-1255 in Australia. In the US, another good source of information is Rail Europe, Tel. 800-438-7245 (toll-free). You can get information from www.raileurope.com or book online at www.trenitalia.com.

Budget Options. If you are planning to include Sicily on an extensive rail tour of Europe, you may want to consider one of the many available types of rail passes. However, since train service is available only in parts of Sicily, don't buy a pass unless you are planning on visiting other parts of Italy and/or Europe as well.

A Eurail pass (available only to travellers who do not reside in an EU country) allows unlimited rail travel through 18 European countries for periods of 15 to 90 days on consecutive passes and 10 to 15 days within a two-month period on the Flexi pass. The pass must be obtained before leaving home. If you are simply interested in getting from one city to another, it may be considerably less expensive to purchase a one-way ticket. For information, in the US contact Rail Europe *(see page 116)*.

A global Inter-Rail pass allows one month's unlimited second-class travel in 30 European countries, including Italy, for residents of the participating countries (for details check <www.interrail.com>). A zonal Inter-Rail card is also available, valid for 16 days travel in Italy, Greece, Slovenia and Turkey.

By Car

Driving to Sicily is a time-consuming proposition. Even from Rome it's a good eight hours to Villa San Giovanni in Calabria, where you'll drive the car onto a ferry for the 20-minute trip across the Strait of Messina. The long journey by car from the UK has become much easier with the launch of the high-speed rail link under the English Channel that connects Folkstone with Calais; cars and passengers are loaded onto a train and whisked through the tunnel in 35 minutes (service runs around the clock with departures every half hour and sometimes more frequently). Speedy as this link is, Sicily is still a long way away from Calais, and a comfortable trip from there will require at least three more days of driving.

By Boat

Ferries run around the clock between Villa San Giovanni near the tip of the mainland to Messina, Sicily's northeastern tip; the trip takes about 20 minutes. There is also frequent hydrofoil service from

Sicily

Reggio di Calabria, a little further south; this trip also takes about 20 minutes. There is also regular service by sea from several other Italian cities: from Naples, daily, about 10 hours, Grimaldi Lines, Tel. (081) 251 4740; from Livorno, three times a week, about 17 hours, Grandi Navi Veloci, Tel. (0586) 829 090; from Genova, daily except Sunday, about 20 hours, Grandi Navi Veloci, Tel. (010) 589 331.

GUIDES AND TOURS *(Guide, Viaggi)*

Guides are readily available in Sicily's cities and at its archaeological sites to provide tours in English. The Italian government tourist office, local tourist offices, travel agencies, and hotels can provide lists. A well-known Italian tour company operating in Sicily is CST, which provides city tours of Palermo as well as tours of the island; Via E. Amari 124, Palermo; Tel. (091) 582 294.

I would like an English-speaking guide.

Ho bisogno di una guida chiparla inglese.

HEALTH AND MEDICAL CARE

You are not likely to encounter any unusual strains of infectious ailments in Sicily, and health care is good. Residents of the EU should carry with them the European Health Insurance Card or EHIC (available in the UK from post offices or online <www.ehic.org.uk>), which entitles them to free medical treatment within the EU. To cover all eventualities, travel insurance is recommended. Non-EU residents are advised to take out a travel insurance policy to cover treatment in Italy. You will often be asked to pay for treatment up front, so keep all receipts for reimbursement.

Pharmacies *(farmacie)* have green cross signs above the entrance; in each town, one pharmacy stays open late and on Sundays on a rotating basis. The after-hour locations for the month are posted in all pharmacies.

Water is considered safe to drink, though like most Italians, Sicilians prefer bottled water, which is very inexpensive. Travellers from abroad may want to follow their example: Water pipes in many cities and towns are very old and impurities may leach in, and spring-fed systems in the country can sometimes be contaminated by animals.

I need a doctor/dentist.	**Ho bisogno di un medico/dentista.**
I have a stomachache.	**Ho il mal di stomaco.**
I have a fever.	**Ho la febre.**
I have sunstroke.	**Ho una colpo di sole.**

HOLIDAYS

Sicily celebrates local festivals throughout the year *(see page 84)*, and all of the national holidays as well. These are:

1 January	New Year's Day (Capodanno)
6 January	Epiphany (Befana)
Spring	Easter Sunday and Monday (Pasqua)
25 April	Liberation Day (Anniversario della Liberazione)
1 May	Labour Day (Festa del Lavoro)
15 August	*Ferragosto* and Assumption Day
1 November	All Saints Day (Ognisanti)
8 December	Day of the Immaculate Conception (Immacolata)
25 December	Christmas (Natale)
26 December	St Stephen's Day (Santo Stefano)

L

LANGUAGE

Most Sicilians are bilingual: They speak Italian and Sicilian, which is a rich blend of Italian and the languages of the various powers who have invaded the island over the centuries; Arabic, French, and

Sicily

Spanish words appear regularly. English is spoken in hotels and restaurants, but once you venture off the tourist track, prepare to communicate in Italian. Don't be shy: Sicilians are very appreciative of foreigners who attempt to speak the language. Some basic tips:

a as in *father*

e as in *egg*

i as *e* in *eat*

o as in *ostracize*

u as *oo* in *mood*

c before *e* and *i* is pronounced *ch,* as in *church.* Otherwise, *c* and *ch* are pronounced *k,* as in *cane.*

g before *e* and *i* is pronounced *j,* as in *gin.* Before other letters, *g* is hard, as in *gun.*

Most feminine words end in *a,* plural *e,* and most masculine words end in *o,* plural *i. La* is the feminine article, *il* the masculine.

Some basic words and phrases:

Good morning/ good afternoon.	**Buon giorno.**	*bwon JOARno*
Please.	**Per favore.**	*pair fahVOAray*
Thank you.	**Grazie.**	*GRAAseeay*
yes/no	**sì/no**	*see/no*
Excuse me.	**Mi scusi.**	*mi skoozee*
Where is…?	**Dovè…?**	*doaVAI…?*
I don't understand.	**Non capisco.**	*noan kahpeeskoa*
open	**aperto**	*ahPAIRtoe*
closed	**chiuso**	*keeOOso*
I'd like…	**Vorrei…**	*vorRAIee*

Numbers:

one	**uno**	seven	**sette**
two	**due**	eight	**otto**
three	**tre**	nine	**nove**
four	**quattro**	ten	**diece**
five	**cinque**	hundred	**cento**
six	**sei**		

Days of the week:

Monday	**lunedì**	Friday	**venerdì**
Tuesday	**martedì**	Saturday	**sabato**
Wednesday	**mercoledì**	Sunday	**domenica**
Thursday	**giovedì**		

MAPS

A good map is handy when you go off the beaten track into Sicily's mountainous interior. Maps of Sicily by Michelin Italiana are excellent, as are those published by the Touring Club Italiano, you can find them in bookstores in Palermo, Taormina and elsewhere.

MEDIA

Some British newspapers are available at newsstands in Palermo and Catania and in the resorts of Taormina and Cefalù. *The International Herald-Tribune,* published in Paris in conjunction with *The New York Times* and *Washington Post and USA Today* are usually available in major cities and resorts; the *International Herald-Tribune* has an excellent daily section devoted to Italian coverage, *Italy Daily,* which is published in conjunction with Italy's leading newspaper, *Corriere della Sera.* In these days of satellite dishes, even small hotels now often provide such English-language television channels as CNN.

Sicily

MONEY

Currency. As of January 2002, the unit of currency in Italy has been the euro, which in general hovers just below or above parity with the US dollar.

Currency Exchanges. Banking hours are generally Monday–Friday from 8:30am–1:30pm and 2:30 or 2:45–3:45 or 4pm, with many exceptions. Major banks in cities and at least one bank in most towns have currency exchanges. Post offices and train stations also usually have currency-exchange windows.

Traveller's Cheques and Credit Cards. Both are widely accepted, though most establishments give an unfavourable exchange rate on traveller's checks; you are better off cashing them at a currency exchange and paying in cash. Visa and Master Card are the most widely accepted credit cards, and many establishments do not take American Express cards.

ATM Machines. ATM machines, from which you can withdraw money in euros from your bank account at home, appear throughout Sicily; most provide instructions in English.

OPENING HOURS

Museums, churches and monuments throughout Sicily are remaining open longer than they once did, often seven days a week and into the early evening. Even so, hours vary widely and many churches throughout Sicily are closed for ongoing renovations; local tourist boards can provide current opening times for sights in a particular town or region. Most sights and businesses close in mid-day for two or more hours. In general, hours are: *banks,* 8:30am–1:30pm and 2:30 or 2:45–3:45 or 4pm, Monday–Friday; *bars,* 7am–11pm, often as late as 2am; churches, very early in the morning until noon or 12:30 and from 3–7 or 8pm (many keep much shorter hours and many are closed to all but mass-goers on Sunday); *museums,* six or seven days a week (many are closed on Sunday), often from 10am–5:30 or 6pm and often with a midday closing from 12:30–3pm; *restaurants,* 1pm–3 or 3:30pm for lunch and from 8–10:30pm for dinner (closed one day a week); *shops,* 8:30 or 9am–1pm and 3:30 or 4pm–7 or 8pm.

POLICE *(polizia)*

There are three kinds of police in Italy: *vigili urbani,* who deal with petty crime, traffic, parking and other day-to-day matters (including the concerns of tourists asking for directions); *carabinieri,* the highly trained national force who handle serious crime and civilian unrest, protect government figures and perform other high-profile tasks; and *polizia stradale,* who patrol the roadways. Any of these forces may answer a 113 emergency call, though the carabinieri have their own emergency number, 112.

Where's the nearest police station?	**Dovè il più vicino posto di polizia?**

POST OFFICES

Post offices are open from 8am–1:30pm Monday–Saturday, and in major cities the main post office is usually open seven days a week from 8am–7:30pm. If you want something to arrive with alacrity, consider using the more expensive Posta Prioritaria. Stamps can be bought in tobacconists *(tabacchi)* too.

Many post offices also send faxes, exchange money and provide public telephones.

I would like a stamp for this letter/postcard.	**Desidero un francobollo per questa lettera/cartolina.**
Airmail	**Via aerea**

PUBLIC TRANSPORT

An extensive network of public transportation makes it easy to move between major cities and towns in Sicily. In travelling around the island, you will use a combination of trains and buses, since many places, especially in the interior and along the southern coast, are not served by train. Ferries and hydrofoils connect ports with the islands.

Tourist offices usually provide train and bus schedules and fare information; in fact, if you explain where you want to go and when, the staff will usually look up times for you. Schedules are posted prominently at train stations. It can be a little more difficult to track down information for an inter-city bus *(pullman)*. In addition to getting information from the tourist office, ask for the *autostazione* (bus station, which is often just a pullover) and look for posted schedules and/or nearby offices of the island's two major bus companies, SAIS and AST. Service is limited on Sundays and, in many cases, after the late afternoon. When travelling by train, you must stamp your ticket in one of the machines on the platform before boarding; you can be fined 50 euros on the spot if you don't.

The main port of the Aeolian Islands is Milazzo, on the northern coast near Messina; boats and hydrofoils run year round between Milazzo and all the islands, with the most extensive service in the summer. Trapani, on the western coast, is the port for ferry and hydrofoil service to the Egadi Islands and Pantelleria.

Palermo, Catania, Siracusa and most towns in Sicily (and even many small towns as well) have excellent bus systems. Tickets can be purchased at newsstands and generally cost one euro. You must stamp your ticket in one of the machines when you board the bus; failure to do so can result in a hefty fine.

When is the next bus/train to…?	**Quando parte il prossimo autobus/treno per…?**
one way	**andata**

roundtrip	**andata e ritorno**
first/second class	**prima/seconda classe**
What's the fare to…?	**Qual è la tariffa per…?**

RELIGION

Like the rest of Italy, Sicily is predominantly Roman Catholic, and Sicilians are more devout than Italians elsewhere. The church, in fact, is still a major part of the community, even in the cities — note the many religious festivals that Sicilians celebrate *(see page 84).*

TELEPHONE *(telefono)*

Public phones in Italy are orange, located all over cities and towns, and take phone cards *(scheda telefonica),* available at tobacco shops and newsagents. To use these phones (which tend to emit an intimidating series of beeps at unexpected times) pick up the receiver, then insert the phone card (phone cards do not work until you rip off the tabbed corner). You will not hear a dial tone — simply dial, and the number you are dialing will appear in a digital display window.

All Italian city codes begin with 0 — a Palermo number begins with 091, not 91. You must precede the number with a city code when dialing from one city to another within Sicily; however, you do not dial a city code when calling within that city (for example, drop the 091 when calling from a number in Palermo to another number in Palermo). To call internationally, you must first dial 00, then the country code (1 for the US and Canada; 44 for the UK; 353 for the Republic of Ireland; 61 for Australia; 64 for New Zealand; 27 for South Africa), then the city or area code, then the number.

Hotels slap very large surcharges on long-distance calls. One way around this is to use a telephone calling card and bill all cards to that. Your calling card company can supply the access code you must dial to reach its system; simply dial the code, and an English-speaking operator will come on to assist you or you can follow a series of English-language prompts.

TIME ZONES

Like the rest of Italy, Sicily is one hour ahead of Greenwich Mean Time (GMT). Italy switches to daylight saving time on the last Sunday in April and reverts to standard time on the last Sunday in October.

New York	**Sicily**	Jo'burg	Sydney	Auckland
7am	**noon**	1pm	9pm	11pm

TIPPING

A service charge of 10–15% is added to most restaurant bills, but even so it is nice to leave a little extra for good service — the amount depends on the total amount of the bill and the quality of the service, but anywhere from 3 to 5 euros is the norm. It's customary to leave a coin or two on the counter for a barman. Tip bellhops a euro per bag. To tip a taxi driver, simply round up the total, but be generous — 5.5 euros becomes 6 euros, for example. Tip guides or coach drivers 5 euros per person.

TOILETS (*gabinetto*)

Public restrooms can be hard to find, and when you do locate one, you usually have to pay to use it. Facilities in train and bus stations often are not well maintained, and the toilets are 'Turkish' (a basin imbedded in the floor, requiring logistics to which many travellers may not be accustomed). For the price of a coffee or a mineral water you can use the restroom in a bar — your best option. The mens' restroom is designated by *uomini or signori,* the ladies' by *donne* or *signore.*

Is it possible to use the bathroom?	**Posso usare il bagno?**
Where are the toilets?	**Dove sonno i gabinetti?**

TOURIST INFORMATION

The place to go first for information is one of the offices of the Italian National Tourist Office (ENIT) in your home country. They can probably supply listings of accommodation throughout Sicily, as well as a wealth of other information. Locations are:

Canada: 175 Bloor Street E, Suite 907 South Tower M4W 3R8 Toronto (Ontario); Tel: 141 6925-4882; fax: 141 6925-4799.

UK: 1 Princes Street, London W1B 2AY; Tel: 0207 408-1254; fax 0207 399-3567.

US: 630 Fifth Avenue, Suite 1565, New York, NY 10011; Tel: 212-245-4822, fax: 212-586-9249.

401 N. Michigan Avenue, Chicago, IL 60611; Tel: 312-644-0990, fax: 312-644-3019.

12400 Wilshire Boulevard, Suite 550 Los Angeles, CA 90025; Tel: 310-820-9807, fax: 310-820-6357.

In addition, many towns have their own tourist offices, which can arrange entry to local events and provide extremely detailed information that often is not available from tourist offices abroad. If you know in advance which cities and towns in Sicily you will be visiting, you may want to write ahead for an information packet or to obtain specific information. Addresses and telephone numbers of some tourist offices (*Informazioni Turistica*) in often-visited towns are: Via C. Battisti 15 **Agrigento**, Tel. (0922) 401-352; Via Cimarosa 10, 95124 **Catania**, Tel. (095) 730-6233; Corso Ruggero 77, 90015 **Cefalù**, Tel. (0921) 421050; Via Guarrasi 1, 91016 **Erice**, Tel. (0923) 869-388; Corso Vittorio Emanuele 202, 98055 **Lípari (Aeolian Islands)**, Tel. (090) 988-0095; Via XI Maggio 100, 91025 **Marsala**, Tel. (0923) 714-097; Piazza Castelnuovo 35, 90141 **Palermo**, Tel. (091) 583-847; Via Sebastiano 43, 96100 **Siracusa**, Tel. (0931) 481232; Piazza Santo Caterina 98039 **Taormina**, Tel. (0942) 23243.

WEIGHTS AND MEASURES

Length

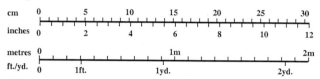

Weight

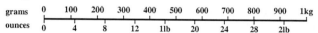

Temperature

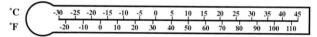

YOUTH HOSTELS

There are a few hostels in Sicily, including ones in Erice and on Lípari in the Aeolian Islands. The Hostelling International Italian affiliate is Associazione Italiana Alberghi per la Gioventù (AIG), which can provide a list of Italian hostels and will book space free of charge. For more information, contact AIG at Via Cavour 44, 00184 Roma; Tel. (06) 487 1152, fax (06) 488 0492. You can also obtain information on Sicilian hostels from the web site of the Hostelling International Association, www.iyhf.org.

Recommended Hotels

Our selective list of hotels below includes those that have a good amount of character, are well-located, provide excellent value for the price, or in some other way are above the ordinary. We welcome your contributions on lodgings that you particularly enjoy.

Reservations are essential almost anywhere in Sicily from May through September, and are highly recommended at other times, especially around European holidays.

As a basic indication of what you can expect to pay, we use the symbols below to indicate prices for a double room with bath, including breakfast. Prices may vary with the season, and some hotels require that guests take meals as well; these pensione plans are usually in effect only in July and August.

€	below 100 euros
€€	100–150 euros
€€€	160–200 euros
€€€€	200–300 euros
€€€€€	300–400 plus euros

PALERMO

Centrale Palace Hotel €€€€€ *Corso Vittorio Emanuele, 90134 Palermo; Tel. (091) 336 666; cphotel@tin.it.* This newly restored hotel in a 17th-century palace just a few steps from the Quattro Canti couldn't be more central. With its nice-sized guest rooms, handsome furnishings and excellent service, the Centrale has also become one of Palermo's better and more stylish hostelries. The rooftop breakfast room overlooks the old city, as do many of the rooms on the upper floors. 63 rooms. Major credit cards.

Grande Hotel e delle Palme €€€€€ *Villa Roma 396, 90139 Palermo; Tel. (091) 602 8111; des-palmes@amthotels.it.* Palermo's famous grand hotel retains its grandeur and charm, making it easy to understand why Palermo society still meets here and celebrities continue to check in (one of the first guests of note was Richard Wagner). The public rooms are ornate and beautifully maintained, and the guest rooms seem to be in a continuous state of renovation — if you don't like the room you are given, ask to see several others because all are different and in various stages of repair; the best are those that retain their high ceilings and fin de siècle furnishings. 192 rooms. Major credit cards.

Tonic €€ *Via Mariano Stabile 136, 90127 Palermo; Tel: (091) 611 1766; www.hoteltonic.com or hoteltonic@hoteltonic.com.* One of the best city bargain lodgings is centrally located. The plainly furnished rooms are comfortable and renovated with style. Major credit cards.

Villa Igiea €€€€€ *Salita Belmonte 43, 90142 Aquasanta, Palermo; Tel. (091) 631 2111; villa-igiea@thi.it.* This art nouveau villa, on the sea just 3km (2 miles) from the city center, provides a perfect retreat in surroundings that were once home to the island's Florio family (of tuna and wine fame). The gardens and sea views are lovely, and amenities include a private beach, swimming pool and tennis courts. The rooms are large and tastefully furnished, and there is an excellent restaurant on the premises. 117 rooms. Major credit cards.

AROUND PALERMO

Mondello Palace €€€€€ *Viale Principe di Scalea, 90139 Mondello; Tel. (091) 450 001; fax (091) 450 657.* Palermo's favourite seaside retreat is the setting for this well-equipped resort, within easy reach of the city centre but offering a pool, beach and other amenities. Rooms are large and very pleasant. 91 rooms. Major credit cards.

AROUND THE ISLAND
AEOLIAN ISLANDS

Gattopardo Park €€€ *Viale Diana, 98055 Lìpari; Tel. (090) 981 1035; gattopardopark@netnet.it.* This 19th-century villa and surrounding bungalows are set in lush gardens, and guest quarters are pleasantly rustic. 53 rooms. Major credit cards.

La Sciara €€€€ *Via Soldato Cincotta, 98050 Strómboli; Tel. (090) 986 004; info@lasciara.it.* This popular summertime retreat offers a vaguely Arabic, whitewashed setting, along with pleasant rooms and a private beach. Services include guided ascents up Strómboli's famous volcano. 60 rooms. Major credit cards.

ARGIGENTO

Concordia €€ *Piazza San Francesco 11, 92100 Agrigento; Tel./fax (0922) 596 266.* One of Agrigento's most popular hotels (and usually booked well in advance) is appreciated for its good value and basic but clean rooms. There's a coffee bar in the lobby, and the hotel owns a fairly priced and quite good trattoria next door, La Forchetta (at which guests receive a substantial discount). 28 rooms. Major credit cards.

Villa Athena €€€€€ *Passeggiata Archeologica 33, 92100 Agrigento; Tel. (0922) 596 288; villaathena@athenahotels.com.* Villa Athena enjoys a location that's sure to win the heart of anyone who can't get enough of ancient wonders — it's set in the Valley of the Temples, surrounded by gardens and olive trees. Guest rooms are comfortably furnished, and some have terraces and astonishing views over the swimming pool and the surrounding ruins. This is one of Sicily's most popular hotels, so it's necessary to book well in advance. 40 rooms. Major credit cards.

CATANIA

Central Palace €€€€€ *Via Etnea 218, 95124 Catania; Tel. (095) 325 344; fax (095) 715 939.* Catania's 4-star hotel is located right in the centre of town and occupies a beautifully restored older building. Guest rooms are large and tastefully furnished, and there is an excellent restaurant and popular bar on the premises. 99 rooms. Major credit cards.

Savona €€ *Via Vittorio Emanuele 210, 95124 Catania; Tel. (095) 362 982; hotelsavona@netnet.it.* This pleasant hotel is in the centre of the old city just off Piazza Duomo. Rooms are large and plainly but comfortably furnished, and the service is excellent; the staff will ensure that you see Catania's considerable sights and will also help you plan excursions to Mount Etna and other places in eastern Sicily. 35 rooms. Cash only.

CEFALÙ

Baia del Capitano €€€ *Contrada Mazzaforno, 90015 Mazzaforno, Cefalù; Tel. (0921) 420 005; www.baiadel capitano.it.* This low-key resort is just outside of town, set in gardens and olive groves above the sea. There's a pool and tennis courts, and the beach is just down the road. 39 rooms. Closed November–February. Major credit cards.

La Giara €€ *Via Veterani 40, 90015 Cefalù; Tel. (0921) 421 562; www.paginegialle.it/hotellagiara.* The setting, right in the middle of the old city, is one of the main draws of this small, family-run hotel. The welcome is warm, and the surroundings, while not luxurious, are pleasing and quite comfortable. A terrace on the roof provides an ideal view over red tile roofs and the duomo. 24 rooms. Major credit cards.

Riva del Sole €€€ *Lungomare Columbo 25, 90015 Cefalù; Tel. (0921) 421 230; lidia@rivadelsole.com.* This centrally located hotel, on the sea just outside of the old town, provides a lot of solid comfort and pleasant furnishings, as well as sea views from many of its rooms. There's a roof terrace and another shady outdoor space in the courtyard. 28 rooms. Closed November. Major credit cards.

EGADI ISLANDS

Aegusa €–€€ *Via Garibaldi 11, 91023 Favignana; Tel. (0923) 922 430; aegusa@cinet.it.* The surroundings at this small hotel are quite tasteful, and the rooms are spacious and comfortable. The Aegusa, in fact, is probably the best the Egadi Islands offers by way of lodging, so you would do well to reserve. 24 rooms. Closed January and February. Major credit cards.

Egadi €€ *Via Colombo 17, 91023 Favignana; Tel. and fax (0923) 921 232.* Reservations are also essential at this modest but comfortable little inn, which is popular with return visitors to the Egadi Islands. Recent renovations have lent the surroundings a contemporary look, but the same family welcome remains. A restaurant on the premises serves meals to guests, who may be asked to opt for full board in August. 9 rooms.

ERICE

Elimo €€€–€€€€ *Corso Vittorio Emanuele 75, 91016 Erice; Tel. (0923) 869 377; www.charmerelax.com.* One of the nicest small hotels in western Sicily is a favourite weekend retreat for residents of Palermo. Rooms are warmly furnished in a smattering of antiques and other traditional pieces, and many enjoy expansive views. If you have one of the viewless rooms facing the courtyard or surrounding streets, you can enjoy the sweeping vistas from the large terrace. 21 rooms. Major credit cards.

Ermione €€–€€€ *Via Pineta Communale 43, 91016 Erice; Tel. (0923) 869 138; fax (0923) 869 587.* The exterior of this 1960s hotel is somewhat worn and bleak looking, but the setting is stunning — right on the edge of a cliff overlooking the sea and plains below. Inside, guest rooms and public areas alike are tastefully decorated and well maintained, and many of the rooms enjoy the views. 46 rooms. Major credit cards.

Moderno €€€€ *Corso Vittorio Emanuele 63, 91016 Erice; Tel. (0923) 869 300; modernho@tin.it.* An excellent restaurant, the best in town, is what draws many people to this tastefully furnished inn. Those who stay on, though, enjoy an unusually attractive, well-run small hotel. The distinctive hand-woven rugs for which Erice is known carpet the halls and some of the guest rooms; other furnishings include pleasant antiques and country pieces, and the views onto the quiet medieval streets are especially moody at night. 40 rooms. Major credit cards.

NOTO

Villa Mediterranea €€ *Viale Lido, 9601 Lido di Noto; Tel. (0931) 812 330; fax (0931) 812 330.* While accommodations in old Noto is hard to come by, you'll find several places to stay in Lido di Noto, on the sea about 6km (4 miles) east. The Villa Mediterranea is one of the most pleasant hotels here, with simple but comfortable modern rooms and airy sea views. 14 rooms.

PANTELLERIA

Port Hotel €€ *Via Borgo Italia 43, 91017 Pantelleria; Tel. (0923) 911 299; porthotel@pantalleria.it.* One of the nicer hotels on the island provides modern comforts in its functional rooms, and has an appealing waterfront location just steps from the ferry dock in the main town. 39 rooms. Major credit cards.

RAGUSA

Montreal €€€ *Via San Giuseppe 6, 97100 Ragusa; Tel. (0932) 621 133; montreal@sicily-hotels.it.* If you want to sleep among the Baroque wonders of Ragusa, you won't find a more central location than this hotel in the busy center. The ambiance leans more towards function than character, but the hotel is within walking distance of the atmospheric old city. Major credit cards.

CAPO SAN VITO

Albergo del Corso €€ *Via Savoia 25, San Vito Lo Capo; Tel. (0923) 972 800; fax (0923) 974 377.* One of many hotels clustered along the finest beach in Sicily, this small inn offers comfortable rooms and fine sea views, along with such welcome amenities as laundry service. 8 rooms. Major credit cards.

SCIACCA

Grand Hotel Delle Terme €€€€ *Via delle Terme 1, 92019 Sciacca; Tel. (0925) 23133; info@termehotel.com.* This elegant seaside hotel carries on an ages-old Sciacca tradition, that of dispensing healing thermal treatments to clientele. Even if you don't require a full regimen, you can enjoy the thermal pool and use the spacious, well-equipped premises as a base from which to explore Agrigento, Sellinunte and other places along the southern coast. 77 rooms. Major credit cards.

SIRACUSA

Gran Bretagna €€ *Via Savoia 21, Ortigia, 96100 Siracusa; Tel. (0931) 68 765; fax (0931) 462 169.* The surroundings are simple but the Gran Bretagna nonetheless attracts legions of return visitors who enjoy the good value and the Ortigia location. Though many of the rooms don't have baths, a few have old frescoes and one has a terrace that looks over rooftops to the sea. 12 rooms. Major credit cards.

Grand Hotel €€€€€ *Viale Mazzini 12, Ortigia, 96100 Siracusa; Tel. (0931) 464 600; www.grandhotelsr.it.* The Grand is the grand hotel on Ortigia, and it is much plusher than its neighbour the Gran Bretagna. In fact, a recent refurbishing left period furnishings and a great deal of style intact, making this the choicest hostelry in Siracusa. Private beach. Major credit cards.

TAORMINA

Mazzarò Sea Palace €€€€€ *Via Nazionale 147, Mazzarò 98030; Tel. (0942) 612 111; info@mazzaroseapalace.it.* One of the most luxurious of the hotels that spread along the sea outside Taormina, the Mazzarò Sea Palace is a distinctive modern property that climbs down a hillside from the coast road; guests enter through the top floor lobby and descend to their rooms, which are commodious, stylishly furnished and face the sea and private beach and pool from large terraces. 88 rooms. Major credit cards.

San Domenico Palace €€€€€ *Piazza San Domenico 5, 98039 Taormina; Tel. (0942) 613 111; san-domenico@thi.it.* A 15th-century monastery manages to retain its austere Renaissance charm while housing one of Italy's most famous and luxurious hotels. Rooms occupy the monks' cells (which have been refitted to provide more spacious accommodation), and are richly furnished; many afford sweeping views along the coast. The chapel is now a bar, while the cloisters remain a peaceful retreat; a swimming pool is set amid the lush gardens. 101 rooms. Major credit cards.

Villa Belvedere €€–€€€ *Via Bagnoli Croci 79, 98039 Taormina; Tel. (0942) 23 791; info@villabelvedere.it.* This lovely hotel is on a view-commanding hillside just above the public gardens, and is set amid its own semi-tropical gardens that surround a lavish swimming pool. Many of the comfortable rooms have balconies, and those in the villa that forms the older section of the hotel are especially atmospheric, with intricate terracotta flooring and antique furnishings. 50 rooms. Major credit cards.

Villa Fiorita €€€€ *Via Pirandello 39, 98039 Taormina; Tel. (0942) 24 122; villafioritahotel@libero.it.* Occupying a large villa near the Greek theater, the Fiorita provides stylish accommodation and such amenities as a garden, solarium and swimming pool. The accommodations are all different, many with stunning views; if the hotel is not full when you arrive, you may want to look around for the room that best suits your tastes. 26 rooms. Major credit cards.

Villa Schuler €€€ *Piazzetta Bastione, 98039 Taormina; Tel. (0942) 23 481; villaschuler@tao.it.* The Schulers have been innkeepers at their ancestral villa for almost 100 years, and continue to provide charming surroundings and the atmosphere of a private home. Most rooms have views down the coast, and the surroundings include a lovely garden and a large, panoramic terrace. Open Easter to October. 26 rooms. Major credit cards.

Recommended Restaurants

Our choice of restaurants includes those that best capture the experience of dining in Sicily while covering a range of prices. Unless indicated otherwise, these restaurants are open for lunch and dinner. As a general rule, this means they serve lunch from 1–3 or 3:30pm, and dinner from 8–10:30pm.

As is the case throughout Italy, a service charge (*servizio*) of 10 or 15% is usually added to the bill. If not, leave a tip of that amount. When a servizio is included, you may want to leave something extra, especially if the service has been attentive and friendly — as it usually is. A euro or two is appropriate, more if the experience warrants it. There will also normally be a *pane e coperto* (bread and cover) charge of a couple of euros.

As a basic guide to what you can expect to pay, we have used the following symbols to give an indication of the price of a three-course meal, excluding wine.

€	below 10 euros
€€	10–20 euros
€€€	20–30 euros
€€€€	over 30 euros

PALERMO

Antica Focacceria San Francesco € *Piazza San Francesco; Tel. (091) 320 264.* For a century and a half, this Palermo institution has been serving tasty, baked-on-the-premises focaccia bread and other tasty snacks from its high-ceilinged, marble-floored location. You can easily assemble a meal from the sandwiches, *arancnie* (fried rice balls) and other fare, and enjoy it in colourful surroundings. Cash only.

Charleston le Terrazze €€€€ *Viale Regina Elena, Mondello; Tel: (091) 450 171.* Although it is on the coast at Palermo's resort of Mondello, this is probably Palermo's most famous restaurant where the smart, fashionable crowds gather, especially in the summer and at weekends. In an art nouveau setting at the water's edge, they serve the finest Sicilian cuisine and the freshest fish. Booking essential. Closed January. Major credit cards.

Pizzeria Bellini €–€€ *Piazza Bellini 6; Tel. (091) 616 5691.* The setting is wonderful — in the arcades of a now defunct theatre and in the shadows of the Norman church of La Martorana — and the fare fits the bill when you are looking for homey Italian cooking. The pizza is thought by many to be the best in town, and pasta dishes are made with sardines, eggplant and other typically Sicilian ingredients. Closed Wednesday. Major credit cards.

Shanghai €€ *Vicolo Mezzani 34; Tel. (091) 589 702.* The fare here is not Chinese — rather, the sea of awnings over the stalls of the surrounding Vucciria market allegedly reminded the owner of the sails of junks in Shanghai harbour. The best time to dine here is in good weather, when meals are served on the terrace. The inexpensive menu is basic, and you are best off avoiding more elaborate dishes and sticking to a plate of simply grilled tuna or swordfish. Closed Sunday. Major credit cards.

AROUND THE ISLAND

AEOLIAN ISLANDS

Da Zurro €€€ *Via Picone, Scari, Strómboli; Tel. (090) 986 283.* This eatery on Strómboli is well known for its fresh seafood dishes and pleasant terrace near the harbour. After enjoying the local catch, accompany one of the delicious desserts with Malvasia, a sweet wine from the neighbouring island of Salina. Major credit cards.

Il Filippino €€€ *Piazza Municipio, Lìpari; Tel. (090) 981 1002.* The best restaurant on Lípari flows out onto a terrace overlooking the main town and harbour. Most of the menu, naturally, comes from the sea, and includes a famous *zuppa di pesce*. Closed Monday and November. Major credit cards.

AGRIGENTO

Caprice €€ *Via Panoramica dei Templi 51; Tel. (0922) 264 69.* This pleasant trattoria is a good place to enjoy lunch while touring the temples, which loom just outside the door. Unlike many restaurants in Sicily, Caprice places an emphasis on meats, which are skewered and grilled, but a wide selection of seafood and pasta dishes is also available. Closed Friday. Major credit cards.

Trattoria dei Templi €€ *Via Panoramica dei Templi 15; Tel. (0922) 403 110.* Fish dominates the menu at this simple, pleasant restaurant that is a neighbour of Caprice *(see above)* in the Valley of the Temples. Closed Sunday and January. Major credit cards.

CATANIA

Costa Azzurra €€€ *Via de Cristoforo 4, Ógnina; Tel. (095) 494 920.* This restaurant at Ógnina, on the beach just north of the central business district, is where Catanians come for excellent seafood meals. The views of the busy harbour are excellent, especially from the terrace. Closed Monday. Major credit cards.

La Siciliana €€€€ *Viale Marco Polo 52a; Tel. (095) 376 400.* Catania's best restaurant is quite a way north of the centre (and expensive by Sicilian standards), but the trip is well worth the effort for the gracious surroundings and excellent menu. The pasta dishes, which rely on such typical Sicilian ingredients as sardines and eggplant, are especially memorable. Closed Monday. Major credit cards.

Pagano €€ *Via de Roberto 37; Tel. (095) 537 045.* Another Catania dining institution occupies solidly old-fashioned quarters in the Excelsior Hotel that have hardly been updated. The menu is traditional, with an emphasis on seafood. Closed Sunday evening and Saturday lunch. Major credit cards.

CEFALÙ

L'Antica Corte €€ *Corso Ruggero 193; Tel. (0921) 423 228.* Fresh fish and pastas topped with seafood-based sauces are favorites on the menu in this old town restaurant. The best seating is in the charming courtyard. Closed Thursday. Major credit cards.

La Brace €€€ *Via 25 Novembre 10; Tel. (0921) 423 570.* Arches and a rough-hewn décor lend ambiance to this pleasant eatery in the old town near the duomo. Grilled meat and fish are a speciality, as are typical Sicilian pasta dishes and such desserts as *cassata siciliana.* Closed Monday. Major credit cards.

ERICE

La Taverna di Re Aceste €€€ *Viale Conte Pepoli; Tel. (0923) 869 084.* The mural-covered dining room provides a cozy, exotic setting. Try couscous (an Arab-inspired speciality in western Sicily) and grilled fish. Closed November. Major credit cards.

Monte San Giuliano €€€ *Vicolo San Rocco; Tel. (0923) 869 595.* A wide selection of Erice specialties, including couscous smothered in a rich fish broth, are served in the medieval courtyard or cozy dining room. Closed Monday. Major credit cards.

NOTO

Trattoria del Carmine €€ *Via Ducezio 1a; Tel. (0931) 838 705.* Friendly surroundings provide a nice lunch stop at Noto on a day trip from Siracusa. Everything here is fresh, homemade and delicious. Such regional specialties as seafood-based pastas are especially good. Closed Monday. Major credit cards.

PIAZZA ARMERINA

Da Totò €€ *Via Mazzini 29; Tel. (0935) 680 153.* This pleasant, family-run trattoria in the heart of Piazza Armerina is an excellent place to stop when passing through town en route to Villa Romana in nearby Casale. The menu reflects the mountain setting, with an emphasis on game, rabbit and other meat dishes. Closed Monday and October through March. Major credit cards.

RAGUSA

U' Saracinu €€ *Via del Convento 7; Tel. (0932) 246 976.* Friendly restaurant considered the best in the old city, located near the cathedral of San Giorgio. The kitchen concentrates on local dishes, accompanied by wines from local vineyards. Closed Sunday. Major credit cards.

SIRACUSA

Archimede €€ *Via Gemmellaro 8, Ortigia; Tel: (0931) 697 01.* Long established restaurant with garden and with a reputation for classic local dishes, especially fish, served at a moderate price. Popular with families. Closed Sundays. Major credit cards.

Don Camillo €€€ *Via Maestranza 96; Tel. (0931) 671 33.* An old Ortigia favourite serves some wonderful variations of local specialties, including pasta with cuttlefish in its own ink or fresh tuna. Closed Sunday, July and November. Major credit cards.

TAORMINA

Granduca €€€€ *Corso Umberto 170; Tel. (0942) 24 983.* The charmingly cluttered, antiques-filled setting offers excellent Sicilian dishes, including homemade pastas topped with rich sauces of eggplant, capers, swordfish and tuna. The views from the glassed-in terrace get rave reviews as well. Closed Tuesday. Major credit cards.

La Botte €€ *Piazza Santa Domenica 4; Tel. (0942) 24 198.* A variety of pasta dishes and excellent pizzas from the wood-burning oven can be had at this pleasant restaurant, with outdoor tables in cobblestoned Piazza San Domenico. Major credit cards.

Vecchia Taormina €€ *Vico Ebrei 3; Tel. (0942) 625 589.* Taormina's most popular casual eatery serves delicious pizza and other light fare for dinner only. Closed Wednesday. Cash only.

INDEX